Bedtime S

for

Tired

Therapists

edited by

Leela Anderson

DULWICH CENTRE PUBLICATIONS
South Australia

Copyright © 1995 by **Dulwich Centre Publications**
ISBN 0 646 23934 1

published by
Dulwich Centre Publications
Hutt St PO Box 7192
Adelaide, South Australia 5000
phone (08) 223 3966

cover artwork by
Mystery of MiskaGraphics, Adelaide, South Australia

printed and manufactured in Australia by
Graphic Print Group, Richmond, South Australia

Contents

Acknowledgements

I wish to acknowledge the mid-wives of *Bedtime Stories*, women whose skills and commitment have assisted its birth and joyful delivery.

Anne Mellor and Jane Hales for their creativity and feet-on-the-ground support with word processing, layout and typesetting. Helen O'Grady and Melissa Raven for their unflappable editorial assistance. And Mystery of MiskaGraphics for her wonderous and celebratory artwork.

Introduction

It has always been a treat for me to escape from the world to read, preferably in bed. The idea of *Bedtime Stories for Tired Therapists* came from my desire to be able to escape at the end of a day and read 'work things' which didn't have to be accompanied by the knitted brows of confusion and a dictionary.

Rather, I wanted to be inspired, touched, and reminded of, not so much the 'how to's' of therapy, but more about the 'why's': why do we work as counsellors, why do we continue to stay working in this field and, given some of its emotional demands, what is it that makes it possible for us to continue with this work?

I also wanted to know and understand how therapy, our meetings with the people who consult us, contributes to and changes our lives. How are we different for the experience and privilege of what we hear and witness? I wanted to read about other therapists' journeys and the ways in which their thinking, their beliefs, their hopes, have been challenged and shaped by this daily interchange. I wanted to read what other workers do when they reach what I call a crossroad of confidence. Was there a connection between these crossroads and when we stopped being aware of and reflecting upon these experiences? Since I couldn't find such a book to take to bed with me, I decided to create one.

Equal numbers of men and women were asked to write, as were people from dominant and non-dominant cultures. In hindsight, I can see that this was not a real offer of equality, and the submitted papers reflect this unintentional discrimination. To write in a language not your own, to write when your cultural traditions are oral, to write exposing your sexuality as other than heterosexual, is to do so with very different personal costs and consequences than for someone to write from the comfort of a dominant cultural position. Understandably, more people from non-dominant cultures declined, and *Bedtime Stories* is emptier for the absence of these voices.

When I approached the contributors of *Bedtime Stories* to write, I knew that I was asking people to travel a public path that is not common in publication, a path that demanded exiting from the six-lane well-signed freeways of academic critique onto the muddy backwaters of the very personal and the less familiar.

Janet Adams-Westcott attached this note to me, along with her first draft of *Ginny*: 'I have never before struggled so hard nor been so discontented with a piece!' We who had the privilege of reviewing Janet's work all wondered what was the source of this discontent. Her piece was beautiful, questioning, compassionate, respectful. And in this description, cradled in those words, we began to touch on the difference, to find a language which made visible what Janet was experiencing: a predicament that I and many of the contributors came to know well, as did those who struggled only to withdraw from the writing because of it.

Words like compassionate, respectful, beautiful, are rarely the words used to describe academic papers. The more familiar route is to express knowing as a theory, to write well referenced by others and with personal detachment. This is also the nucleus of what is often considered professionalism.

In contrast, to make space, to even sanction, as *Bedtime Stories* does, personal experience and self-reflection as an important, different kind of knowing, is to ask writers *and* readers to travel into new territory. This journey requires us to see with new eyes, calls for our ears to detect and appreciate the foreign sounds of uncertainties, and challenges us to experience the discomfort that comes with the realisation that the magic of a particular event cannot automatically be applied to another, nor generalised to become a theory.

When I read papers that suggest that the author has *always* thought and worked in a certain way, I often feel cheated by the printing of such a solitary and often sterile single frame, when what I really want is to see the whole movie. With this in mind, I asked each contributor to consider her/his own 'movie', to include in their paper the journey of their changing practices: how and why their ideas and ways of working had shifted from A to B to C ... to Z and beyond into their own alphabet. It has been wonderfully liberating and a rare experience for me to read therapists' reflections and discussions about some of their blind spots and some of the not-so-useful ways of working, and how they began to dissect and dismantle the A's and the B's to create other practices which were more in tune with their evolving values and ethics. When we are willing to include these parts of our working history, we no longer have to defend the claim of 'having arrived', but can languish in some more restful yet effervescent place of always 'becoming'. Subsequently, not all the papers are soft and dreamy bedtime stories. Some reflect more the 'grim fairy tales' that can also be a part of our day-to-day working lives. Stories of how we rise to meet those situations and the human ways in which we falter and yet, often against the odds, move forward, are equally significant in their insightfulness and are welcome 'stories'. Other pieces raise important dilemmas, insist on space for contraditions and, in the 'true' spirit of post-modernism, they evoke more questions than answers.

While few contributers would describe themselves as exclusively 'narrative therapists', each person has been interested in and influenced by the ideas of narrative therapy; all work in ways that value and pursue social justice.

Finally, I wanted to speak to the idea that it is not only the therapists who give out, that this work is not a one-way process. What becomes so clear in the experiences of all who have written is that the alchemy is reciprocal, and that we too are changed. The birth of such transitions is not always joyful nor pain-free; sometimes we too are broken open. Different, enriched, enraged, inspired, the who that we become is often profoundly altered by the meetings we have with those with whom we work. *Bedtime Stories* is an opportunity for me and others to acknowledge that debt. Andrea rieniets, in her song, *Souvenir*, writes about how we have to 'give something back'. *Bedtime Stories* is about giving something back to the people with whom we work.

Leela Anderson, Editor
January 1996

Souvenir
for Claire

you can take my photo but you've got to give
something back
you can take my story but you've got to give
something back
you can take my time, think you can take
what's mine
but you'll find it's no wonder you find the rug
pulled out from under you
you can take it real easy but you've got to give
something back

we can take it over but we've got to give
something back
we can take it as given but we've got to give
something back
we can take it well or we can take it so hard
to find the family tree got planted in someone
else's yard
we can take offence (a fence) but we've got to give
something back

you can take me on but you've got to give
something back
you can take me down but you've got to give
something back
if you find the cause to love what's yours
in the sweet ache of the open palm
you'll catch a glimpse of the celestial charts
you don't have to take this, you can give
something back

Fluently helvetica (compact disk). Lyrics & vocals: Andrea reiniets.
Produced by Michael Turrell. Co-produced by Andrea reiniets.
Re-printed with permission: Independent Distributors, Gouger St PO Box 10059, Adelaide, South Australia.

Leela Anderson

'Leela' is a chosen name of some ten years. It has two meanings. It means *to play*, however, it has two translations: the first is *playful* - to live with joy and exuberance; the second is *to play my part* - to not slide away from the difficult and the hard work of painful things. It is a constant challenge to keep both meanings alive and to find the balance between the two.

It is interesting for me to reflect on the ideas that run through the following pieces, eight vignettes, 'windows' of my work. Each was written separately, each began as a moment that I wanted to record without fully understanding its significance. Despair, respect, hope and change seem to be the recurring themes, and perhaps they are the key ways in which this work affects me, why I was attracted to it in the first place, why I stay. Each theme has a history in my life, each has shaped and continues to shape the person that I am now; all will signpost, in their own way, the yet unspoken and the unseen of my future.

When Words Are Not Enough

Today I called them magicians. Exhausted, deeply sad, they sit, turned slightly away from each other, bewildered like deer in a spotlight. Yet theirs is not the fright of innocence, it is the look and the horror of knowing you have been dragged back into a familiar hell-hole that you thought you had escaped. They have been back in court. On trial for an entire day, with lawyers attempting to assassinate their characters; all the while their rights to parent dangling precariously before them.

L and D are two women, partners of five years, parenting L's two boys. L's ex-partner, the boys' father, has used his enormous wealth, his personal army of barristers, his access to technology, his certainty as a man, to defend again, not his desperation to parent his children, but his 'manhood' in response to 'his' wife being lesbian and loving a woman. There is, perhaps for the first time in his life, nothing he can do to change a situation. This sense of powerlessness seems to have unleashed a wrath, a venom which pours forth over the family I am working with, poisoning the water from which they have little choice but to drink daily. There seems no antidote available, only the magic they weave between them, the loving and intimacy they describe as something neither of them has ever experienced before with another.

I know that over the last year I have become a part of their defence team, a witness to their courage, testimony to the endurance of their love. Yet today, silently, I too joined the fear, had glimpses of the damage these battles are doing to their sense of future: how guilt is having L withdraw because she doesn't want to subject D to this anymore, how D is losing her sense of a life beyond struggle and conflict.

It is times like this that I lose faith in my beloved words, which have for me almost always carried with them the hope that, if they are used well, with love and respect, change is possible. In situations like this I want to abandon the world of words. I feel angry at my naiveté in thinking that words are enough. I want to depart from polite protocol. I want to become a terrorist with weapons stronger than speech. I want to be like a founding member of the Vancouver Greenpeace, who left that organisation to become a pirate, whose sea missions of direct action literally ram environmental trespasses with 20 tons of reinforced steel - I want to do that instead of talking!! I want the sign outside my office building to read 'Pirate Therapist in Revenge Therapy'!!

I know the consulting work I do 'behind closed doors' is political, that it does challenge the oppressive aspects of dominant cultural ideas, and that it can facilitate change. However, working with people like L and D does jolt me into questioning whether I really do believe that words are enough. And I think my answer is 'No'. Not that I have to reject words as useless or invalid or the enemy of action, but I do think I/we as practitioners have to find ways to go beyond the separateness of our individual work and agitate for broader change: how we present or organise conferences; the ways we work with colleagues; the setting up of accountability structures to the people we are working with; or change at a broader community level of social action, which can, for example, challenge the legal structures that allow and therefore support the terrorising of women like L and D. Hope is fragile and mine fluctuates daily.

P.S.:

L and D won that court battle, but none of us is living in the illusion that it will be their last.

Men In Grey Suits

To my despair, most of the important decisions in the world, like nuclear testing in the Pacific, defence budgets, access to health and education, are still being made by white men in grey suits. Of course some women are squeezing into this attire too, and not all men in grey suits are on the same team. However, the daily news captures this power night after night on television, a phenomenon which seems almost immutable.

Working with men like Mark helps me to hold onto the hope that change is possible, that men can challenge their suited destiny and embrace life-sustaining ways. These new ways appeal to me because they seem to offer a type of protection to the planet, and to me as an individual woman, which is based not on the more traditional male ways of patronisation, but on a form of protection based on connection.

I first met Mark when I was consulting at a non-government agency which offered general and relationship counselling. He was clearly in pain when he moved to get out of the waiting-room chair, and when he sat, this time in my office, I saw that his shoulders were quite twisted and his right arm and wrist muscles atrophied, the skin on his hands shiny. (I am often grateful for my original training as a physiotherapist because I still retain a curiosity and watchfulness of the body, not in a way that is interested in interpreting body language, but in a way that acknowledges that people's stories are not separate from a physical 'home' called the body.)

Mark began to talk about his current situation, of being 36 and forced by his recent ill-health to leave both his work and his female partner in Japan and to return to Australia. Mark was now significantly dependent upon his parents, not only for a place to live, but often for his basic day-to-day physical care. Mark described his current physical state as a relapse, the origins of his condition dating some 10 years back. He said that the reason he was seeking counselling was that he wanted to pursue the possible 'psychological component of his illness' as well as ways of dealing with the disability. He added, tentatively, that he also wanted to look at his relationships with women which, in his words, had always been disastrous.

What we began to explore in that meeting and the dozen or so which followed was not in itself extraordinary: the effects and changes the pain was having on his life; how he and others viewed his disability, his sense of future, etc.; and how his illness impacted upon his experience of himself as a man.

What was extraordinary, however, was that I think Mark was the first man whose experience of *being a man* I genuinely and wholeheartedly sought to know and understand. I write this with some sense of disquiet, that it might seem a strange thing to have a noticeable and obvious marking point at which, as a counsellor, I was available to another person's story.

Reviewing my work history helps me to place this shift in context.

Prior to this position, I had worked at a women's community health centre for seven years and, although I had worked with male partners of women using the services, I predominantly worked with women. The majority of these women were dealing with both past and present violence and abuse by men, and their lives in a working-class community were constantly being passed over, yet affected, by 'men in grey suits'. There had been little opportunity or grounds for desire on my part to explore 'men's experiences' when I was dealing on a daily basis with the often life-threatening effects of 'men's behaviour' on women and their children.

So what was it about Mark and our relating which contributed to this new opening of understanding in me? As we talked, I think I recognised in Mark the potential grey suited-destiny that his (our) class and white culture had preplanned for him, and I respected the deliberate choices he had made to be a different kind of man. These choices were not without costs to his material lifestyle and had created at times a sense of uncertainty as to what it meant for him to be a man. For many years he had challenged disconnection at a more global level, using his educational opportunities to work with a national peace action organisation. Now he spoke of wanting to extend this path of connection to his personal life.

For me, working with Mark meant many things. It meant putting aside the belief that I knew his motivations. It meant scowling at the inclinations I had to simplify his actions and intentions, and being open to the uncomfortableness of contradictions. It meant trusting that I was a respected party in the dialogue and not an object to be used, someone to collude with him at the expense of women. It meant being willing to face my unwillingness to learn from men's experiences and to see these experiences as separate from men's theories of knowledge. It meant no longer having a defined place to situate men as other, foreign, perpetrator.

When I try to understand how and why these shifts in me were possible at that time, I am reminded of a phrase that Johnella Bird used during a recent workshop. The group was discussing the impact of taking an expert position on our work versus therapists 'being available to their own surprise'[1].

Since that conversation, I have been trying to figure out what promotes my own 'availability to surprise'. I think there are probably many ingredients, but, in reviewing my work with Mark, respect feels central. Mutual respect seems to foster goodwill, room to move, almost a physical softening, a letting-go in me. I don't think it is as possible for me to make another person's experience invisible when it is illuminated by a backdrop of respect. What that backdrop in turn makes more visible to me, more tangible, is a sense of 'Behold: spirit', a place from which I am more able to see a person's spirit as separate from their beliefs and destructive or negative ways of being.

There were many things to respect about Mark: his willingness to question and to be open to unpleasant answers; his dogged investigation of the notion that his value as a man was based on achievement, and the impact this belief had on his relationships with women; the telling of his shame at being dependent upon his partner; ways of behaving with women that he regretted; his decision to develop a different kind of strength that moved away from dealing with hurt in isolation towards a strength that comes from connecting with others.

I also respected Mark's commitment to put into everyday practice some of the ideas we discussed in session. One meeting he reported that he was trying the idea of lying on his bed and only when he was really clear about what he felt he needed to do to support his body, would he act. Sometimes this meant he would lie down for several hours, deciphering and decoding 'the shoulds, the having to achieves', before he felt that he could hear another voice, another kind of inner knowing.

Mark said that he had begun to understand and realise that 'connection is a process, not an end product'. No longer wanting to be defined by what he achieved, even within the peace movement, Mark stated that he was 'ready to live with the tension of having an unknown destiny' - and we discussed his need for a new passport!

At our meetings I began to notice that the size of Mark's carry-packs was increasing with each visit, and then one day the bike helmet appeared! Mark was riding a bike after eleven years of not doing so, was also now able to swim eight laps. I had been only ever a small part of his team. He had a supportive doctor, a wise and thought-provoking masseur, and, most importantly, Mark had a quality of determination which helped him to maintain, over the months, a vision that he could be a different kind of man.

Nine months after our original meeting, we sat for an acknowledged last session. Amid the discussion and reflections of our time together, Mark ventured a challenge to me, in the shape of a question: 'So, when are you going to start looking after yourself?'

I'm meeting with Mark next week over coffee, so he can review this paper. I can tell him that I've rejoined the gym, found a yoga class which is almost exclusively in the supine, and I (mostly) no longer work until 8 pm. I think he'll be pleased that I too am beginning to peel back the tentacles and challenge the grip of this 'grey suited' idea that I am only what I can achieve.

Louise

I had worked with many women in similar situations but there was something about Louise that pulled at my heart. Perhaps it was her youthful vulnerability - 18 seems such a long time ago for me; perhaps it was something about the way she looked, mirroring my own darkness, my roundness; perhaps it was the imprisonment of her spirit by a culture tight with rules for 'its' women; or perhaps she became the collective force of all women who do not fit in. Whatever the reasons, there was a tenderness which guided my explorations, a more than usual carefulness of the words I chose. I remember wondering, in the beginning only to myself, what it was like to be 18 in 1994 and thinking you might be lesbian? I too had considered the same question at 18, except it had been 1974 in what were very different political times.

Louise was living at home with her parents, who had immigrated from Italy to Australia before she was born. From a working-class background, Louise was the first of her siblings to be studying at university. Family life and acceptance were of central importance to her, as was her belief in God and the Catholic Church. Cultural expectations that Louise would live at home until she married were, at least in her parent's eyes, taken for granted, as was the regular parading of suitable young men whom she was expected to date. No one knew about Louise's inner turmoil. She spoke of her sexuality as 'weird, disgusting, unworthy of God's love'. As the weeks passed, the depression she was experiencing was threatening her ability to study, and failure would mean she would lose financial government assistance.

Her complete isolation used to throw me. Often there is one person in an adolescent's life, dead or alive, who might not totally reject them for their sexuality. Through that person, even if contact remains imaginary, there is a chance to mirror another impression that counters the isolation, the loathing and self-hatred. But for Louise there seemed to be no-one. Catholic school teachers, God, parents, friends, neighbours, all, she felt, would denounce her. I used to work so hard! OK ... well, what about the world of ideas and philosophy that she was studying, perhaps here there was room for difference to be acceptable or even celebrated? Maybe ... We moved slowly. I worried about her safety. I remember inviting her to ask me questions about my own journey, stepping over a line I would not normally cross, anything to help keep her connection with herself, her spirit for life. (In Australia, 33% of cases of youth suicide are thought to be sexuality related [Penley-Miller[2]].)

It was Louise's isolation and her need for contact with the 'Lesbian Community', outside the gaze of her family and culture, which made me determined to revive an idea for which I had been trying to secure funding over the years. I wanted to set up a 'buddy' system whereby volunteers from the gay and lesbian community would provide peer support for people newly identifying as gay or lesbian. It needed funds to co-ordinate, and the only organisations which were willing to support the idea had no money. However, it was 1994, which made it ... The International Year of the Family! Invitations from my work-place management went out to workers to submit proposals for suitable family projects. I spoke to a friend and co-worker about the buddy idea, saying to her, 'I know they'll never fund this, and it will be a mad push to get up yet another submission that will go nowhere, but I want to stick it in their faces that "we" have families too!' - an ever so grown-up motive! coupled with hidden hope that something would come of it for Louise and the many other women and men like her.

We had the usual time of less than a week to get the submission together and then - we waited - for the ripples to tidal wave down from executive-third floor to the coun-selling services on the first ... and, to my shock, the waves never came. We never even got wet, although I suspect our manager did as she went into the swim for *us*. B-Friend is now up and running, even though Louise decided that, by the time it was operational as a scheme, she didn't really need to be involved.

Miracles do happen, mostly outside of the therapy room, and Louise's came in the form of her 20-year old cousin, David. They had been close years earlier and she was desperate to break free of the suffocation and the secrecy. When she told him about her sexuality, he was very quiet and reserved, which understandably she took for rejection. However, he was gathering strength to tell her that he was gay!

Louise and I continued to meet, although less regularly, to discuss her concerns about her family, her future, her adventures with David, who by then had a boyfriend. No longer totally isolated, she saw a light at the end of the tunnel, and she had her own torch.

After our last meeting together, I returned from lunch to a basket of dried flowers on my desk, a present from Louise. I was touched by her gift, especially since I knew that, on a student's budget, it would mean going without other things. But her gift also plummeted me back to the memory of my own parting from Viv, the first therapist I had worked with as a client when I was about 23. Even at that age, symbols and rituals of acknowledgement had been important to me and I too had given her a bunch of dried flowers. I remember saying to Viv that they represented the 'everlasting gifts' she had given to me. Standing in my office, I knew I had made a difference to Louise's life, that there had been an important exchange of everlasting gifts between us, and how many people can go home knowing that?

The following words are from Kaye, a woman with whom I had been working, and, although they are her words in a letter to me, they capture a reciprocal feeling of how I am affected by the work. The 'bit' Kaye chased up was in response to my vague grappling for the memory of this poem, which summarised the journey I felt Kaye had been on (I can never remember who wrote what book or who directed what film). I now know, thanks to Kaye, that 'bit' is T. S. Elliot:

Dear Leela,

I'm sure we're often changed by our encounters with others, sometimes profoundly. I feel enriched by having shared fragments of my life with you. I seem to have rediscovered my essential joy in being, for now at least, and who can ask for more than that? I value your part in that rediscovery and in the exploration of new possibilities of being, of my being. Thank you.

And I found the bit. Good old T.S.E.
We shall not cease from exploration
And the end of all our exploring
Will be to arrive where we started
And know the place for the first time.

Therapeutic Festivals

I can only assume that other workers who work in human services amid social injustice have a variety of ways of dealing with the pain of what they hear and witness daily - talking with co-workers and reminding themselves of the hope that much of the work generates, fitness of endless combinations, yoga, meditation, 'a life' outside work, a variety of substances and other distractions, not to mention family and friends. Usually one or a combination of these strategies is enough to counter-balance some of the strongly disturbing experiences I hear in the everydayness of my work.

However, some days (usually 'some nights') none of these efforts is enough to quell the waves of feelings that I experience for the people I have been with, for the torturing of their bodies and their spirits, for the knowledge that it is still going on. Recently I have added weeping to my pool of survival strategies. I used to fight these tears, see them as signs of giving up, of it all getting too much, and that perhaps I should change jobs. But now I am becoming more comfortable about them when they appear, these determined if uninvited evening guests.

Michael Leunig is an Australian cartoonist, whose soft and exceptional illustrations capture his unique window of humanity. I am especially fond of his series *Festival of Sobbing and Weeping* in which he depicts a variety of ways and places in which humans cry: solo, in groups, suburbia, and in the wild. In the past my personal favourites have been the 'Nocturnal dog weeping' and the 'Deep rhythmic urban carpet sobbing'. However, I think Leunig might well be envious of my recent discovery of a new entrant, one that, to my knowledge, he has not pencilled into his 'festivals'. I think it should be called the 'too hot bath crouching sobbing', and it probably will appeal to people like myself who feel most at home not on land but in the water ...

Rarely - but still it happens - my work has me returning home with very little energy to feed myself, or to do anything but crawl into a bath; and it was on one such recent occasion that I discovered the versatility of these uninvited guests. No water restrictions here; the bath is overflowing. I know that the water is too hot, but even so this information does not impact on my desire to be weightless, to be immersed, so I step in, two feet. Caught. It is clearly physically fatal to move further into the water, and emotionally terminal for me to step out of the bath, so in this state I discover that it is possible to crouch sideways and lean against the coldness of the tiles and, there, crouched, weep.

Not that difficult to reproduce and, with room for individual flare and bath size, it is a survival strategy that I imagine may have widespread appeal.

A creature of habit, I will probably always lean towards the deep rhythmic urban carpet sobbing; however, it was especially comforting to be able to weep in my home, the water.

No Time To Grieve

I had been saying why I had decided to leave the women's health centre and work for myself ...

Political and economic rationalism was about to change the face of women's and community health services forever. I had moved states some 12 years earlier, specifically to work in Adelaide and community health, in what was then considered to be one of the most radical and progressive places. To now stay and see it all dismantled seemed too hard ... the crisis nature of the work ... feeling like I rarely went home with a sense of completion, never clearing my desk with space for tomorrow without going in early to deal with yesterday ... how years of being the 'keeper of other people's secrets'[3] and horror takes its toll - lots of things contributed to my decision, but I always seem to gloss over Terry. Not that she caused me to leave, but my work with her unlocked a door I could not close. As I try now to understand my decision to move on, I see my connection with Terry as a turning point in my own recognition that I needed to go, even if it would be nearly six months before I actually left.

Terry approached the centre about her husband's violence, which she said she had tolerated until he had began to hit out at their three preschool children. The violence quickly escalated as soon as he became aware of Terry's stand for the safety and protection of herself and her children. Within a matter of weeks Terry's situation was highly dangerous and she decided to leave her home. Emergency shelters, half-way housing, it didn't seem to matter where Terry tried to hide, he found them. She felt that there seemed little option but to go interstate, to change her name, to try to outrun him. Terry's sister, Karla, was the only other person who knew what was happening. It was painful for Karla to hold up the mask of pretence, while all the time supporting Terry, who was also moving out of her life. We organised the place, the day and the time and she did it without a hitch. I never heard from Terry again. I got news from Karla a few weeks later that they were all OK.

Other work took over for me. About a year later I got a call from reception. I remember that I was about to facilitate a group, because I said I'd take the call later, but no, it was urgent. It was STD. It was Karla, and Terry was dead. She had successfully escaped her husband's violence, only to be killed by her new male partner. How to write about both the shock of such a death, and it was not a totally foreign work experience for me - I had worked in a hospice years earlier where unexpected and violent death had happened. What was equally shocking as hearing about Terry's death was that there seemed no time to register her death, the meaning of her life to me, no time to grieve.

After hanging up the phone from Karla, I did the group, got caught on the stairs afterwards by someone who needed to talk about something she couldn't say in front of the group; downstairs, a pigeon-hole full of messages, closed doors, co-workers busy, no-one available. Someone in crisis walks in off the street and I'm on roster. I remember going upstairs and throwing something across the room in a fit of rage and frustration, that there was 'never any bloody person around this place when you need them and no time even if someone is free!' It sounds pretty melodramatic: why couldn't I have just cancelled something, made space, insisted on time with a fellow worker? This was not an uncaring or insensitive work-place. I had never worked with such a wonderfully committed and passionate group of women.

The mad pace of ten things in your head at any given time, the feeling that we never really finished at the end of the day, the constant rationalising of who was most 'needy' because we couldn't do it all, set up a sort of work ethos that I shake my head at now trying to describe. If there was no time to grieve for such a brutal and graphic loss, what did this mean for the many smaller 'deaths'/losses which I and others experienced every day? What effect was this lack of opportunity to reflect on my work, my ideas, my responses having on me? What was the cost of pretending that I didn't need it, and that action and 'doing' were consistent priorities over self-reflection and 'being'?

The closed-door intimacy of counselling is not one-way, even if the exploration is only on behalf of one person. I too am affected by the exchange, and it seems both a waste and a disrespect to that interchange not to insist on time to honour it, to learn from it, and be different for the meeting.

Working for myself makes this process more possible, although it requires discipline and finding colleagues who are equally committed to these values. I am excited by the recent setting up of fortnightly peer supervision with someone who shares my belief that there needs to be such a balance.

I feel incredibly grateful for those seven years, and hold impossible and probably slightly romanticised criterion from which I judge commitment and passion for work, feel guilty that I've got off the boat, admire friends who have stayed to continue the fight, miss terribly the camaraderie.

If Only I Had More Skills

Counselling invites, if not demands, stillness from me. Several years ago I attended a workshop facilitated by Amanda Kamsler, a Sydney-based therapist, who spoke of the idea of how narrative therapy requires us to 'traffic in uncertainty'. When I heard this phrase, I felt such an 'Ahah!', a sitting-forward in my body, a 'Yes!' to this phrase which captured some of my experience of this way of working. I am aware that 'trafficking in uncertainty', remaining open to the 'not knowing' inherent in uncertainty, demands a stillness in me. I ask myself, 'what do I mean by the word stillness?' This word reflects the quality of what I feel and yet its meaning is vague. I have a better sense of what it *doesn't* mean: for me it doesn't mean a nothingness, a clean slate void of ideas or knowledge. Nor does it mean being unaware of my experiences, of either what is transpiring between myself and the person I am working with or my past experiences.

Stillness seems to be something more akin to a preparation for receptivity to my thoughts and feelings where I *know* them to be just that, *my* thoughts and feelings, which may or may not be useful in the conversation; a place from which I can respond, without assuming I know. Yet my idea of receptivity is not about passivity, rather more the kind of receptivity I see in my cat as he watches and waits in preparation for responding (unfortunately to birds), a state which is invisible, still, yet intensely active. As I try to articulate this experience of stillness, I am reminded of its parallels to meditation.

I have been interested in meditation off and on for 20 years, or, perhaps more accurately, my interest has always been 'on' and my practice has been erratically 'off and on'. My teacher has encouraged a celebration of life and playfulness, which extended to his meditation methods: some very active, physical with dance and music; others more traditional, in silence, watching my breath ... journeying, observing my thoughts ... then becoming my thoughts ... and then, arr ... back to watching my breath. Whatever the method, all have been clear invitations for me to watch my thoughts, my feelings, my beliefs, whatever these may be at a particular time, and to see them as just that, and not the 'truth' of who I am. He also spoke of meditation as being something beyond monastic mountain-sitting, something we should practice in the market-place of everyday life.

In recent years I have had conversations with friends who are also therapists, about how I experience narrative therapy as a 'living market-place meditation', a way for us (both client and therapist) to separate ourselves from those ideas which speak to us as our 'true selves'. We do this through externalisation/watching, whereby we begin to deconstruct the 'truths' of the 'I' we have been encouraged to believe that we are.

The effect of this process on me is that it is like meditating for eight hours each day. It offers me the challenge of extricating myself from my particular thoughts and feelings, and to engage in a living conversation, a dialogue out of stillness and an openness to the not knowing, to this process of 'trafficking in uncertainty'. Of course, anybody who has tried to meditate would be smiling at this point, because to experience this stillness, this place of receptivity, is an exasperating and demanding process. I often feel that the words 'just sit' should never be allowed to be written in close proximity to each other because they are a paradox in themselves! Yet, as in meditation, the quality of the experience of my work is significantly enriched when I am able to 'just sit', to receive and respond from this place of stillness.

While there are many things which move me out of stillness, lately I have been collectively summarising them as *despair* and *desire*. The voice of despair articulates ideas that range from the local level - 'I don't know enough, if only I had more skills' - to the more global position of 'The world's doomed and what good does talking do anyway?' Equally, despair will disconnect me from stillness by teaming up with the other person's sense of hopelessness and this reinforces and confirms the original despair of 'If only I had more skills'!

Desire is another entity altogether. It teams up with an overly developed sense of responsibility and robs me of stillness by encouraging me to believe that I know what the person I am working with 'should do'. Alternatively desire has me wanting to prematurely open up conversations which will highlight a person's beauty and the power of their own spirits. I have a cartoon I use for teaching which illustrates this common desire in action. Picture two mountains, one client climbing the nearest mountain, one therapist forging ahead on the distant mountain. The therapist has a megaphone and is calling back to the client 'Your alternative story is over here!' Desire is big on megaphones.

These internal conversations of desire/despair do not, of course, occur separately from the concurrent external conversation happening in the room. In fact, some external conversations have an enormous capacity to turn up the volume of my internal conversations, drowning out any ability I have to create stillness.

The impact of some of these 'rowdy' conversations was made clearer to me following a consultation I sought with Michael White and a reflecting team. It highlighted a previously unknown aspect of my work which has given despair/desire a major foothold in my work without my having been aware of its presence.

I wanted to explore the role of respect in couple relationships. What happens to the couple's relationship when there isn't respect, and what impact does disrespect have on the therapeutic relationship, on my work and on how I experience myself as a therapist?

The discussion began by my reviewing two separate experiences I had had in working with couples. The first couple were well practised in adversarial ways and had openly engaged in exchanges of disrespectful hostility in front of me. The second experience, which occurred on the same day, provided a strong contrast. It was a session in which the conversation and exploration of the problems were supported by the couple's sense of responsibility and respect. How I experienced myself as a worker was quite different in those different environments, even though the presenting problems were not dissimilar. Respect seemed to hold some key to my understanding of the 'why'.

What became clear to me was that when there is disrespect and open hostility, I get caught up in the same system - I take less risks, I'm less creative; I go into what feels like robot mode, reverting to the first questions I ever learnt. My ability to be still and to self-reflect freezes over and refuses to melt, despite the rapidly rising room temperature. I often think that in moments like this, if my chair had coasters on it, I'd be noticeably rolling backwards! It is at this point that I am most likely to believe the idea that 'If only I had more skills, then this wouldn't be happening.'

As we continued to talk I was shocked to hear myself saying something that I had never thought of before. When I witness people treating each other with anger and without respect, I see them as engaging in a process of disconnecting from their own humanity. I then went on to disclose that somehow, in this situation, I felt responsible for re-connecting them with their humanity (which is a bit of a task really, and requires a permanent set of Wonder Woman wings!).

Even I can recognise this as a ludicrous and ridiculous expectation. While I had been aware of the general colour of 'over-responsibility' in my life, I was a stranger to this particular mutation until this conversation. I know its history but I also know that is not my present. Once brought into the light, this expectation seemed to just dissolve. I now rarely feel, and then only in diluted version, this dynamic in my couple work, even when there is an atmosphere of disrespect. I am more aware that my experience of myself as a worker is contextual and not some constant that remains unaffected by the environment in which I am working. I think this has always been clear to me in contexts of other strong emotions, e.g. sadness, pain, fear, but such was the disguised power of this expectation that I thought I should be unmoved and unaffected by anger, hostility and disrespect. Now the voice of despair, 'If only I had more skills', has one less line in its vocabulary, one less megabyte of power in the PC of my mind.

Since that consultation, it has also been useful for me to track the importance of respect/disrespect in my own life, to look at ways I might be able to bring the second 'respectful' couple onto my imaginary team when working in adversarial atmospheres, and to consider how I might be able to identify the tactics of disrespect earlier so that I can recognise and intercept the robot mode of working.

Equally important now is both my desire and commitment to not leave myself out of the emotional stage upon which hostility and disrespect are playing, and to find ways of naming the impact that these ways of relating have on others, myself included.

Ordinary Days Of Our Lives

When Vanessa Swan suggested that we present together, inwardly I jumped at the chance. I loved working with her and it also provided me with a way of presenting in a larger arena than I was used to, yet with her familiar support - which meant there was even a chance that it could be fun!

Vanessa suggested that, since we both worked extensively in the area of child sexual assault (CSA), perhaps we could present on some aspect of that work. Mmm ... it didn't grab me. I remember thinking that I currently had nothing to say about CSA, except maybe how I manage to keep one step ahead of my clients' own despair, the learning of patience, the valuing of the part the therapeutic relationship played - nothing outstanding enough to do a paper or a workshop, nothing worthy of a public presentation at an international conference.

I came home and niggled away at my own discomfort at what I had said. What constitutes the noteworthy? What did it say that I didn't think that the days of my (work) life were important and that nobody else, I presumed, would be interested in the nitty-gritty of my/the everyday?

The word that I began to play with was *ordinary*. Where was the place for the recognition of the ordinary? How had it been relegated, in my mind at least, to the world of less than, only one step ahead of failure? Had it suffered an unfair fate by being coupled with *mediocre*? How had the unique, the special, the extra-ordinary managed to fill centre stage, not even leaving room in the wings for its counterpart, ordinary? What happens to our work and to us individually when we only attend to or search for the extraordinary?

I was reminded of a small brooch a friend had made for me, a round and voluptuous silver tea-pot, with a golden heart in the middle of it. This gift symbolised a passing comment I had made about the meaning of connection in my life: how I thought all acts of revolution, perhaps particularly in women's lives, whether they be political or of the heart, began over a cup of tea. Somehow the birth of connection is, for me, in the ordinariness of acts like the sharing of tea.

I began then to wonder if we don't share a lot of similar moments of connection in our work, that go unnoticed by us, yet I suspect are significant and foundational to those we work with.

The extraordinary, the unique, the outstanding, are all words which are used to herald what it means to be a successful person in my white western culture. Ordinary seems to have shrunk under the constant scrutiny and harassment of individuality. I think ordinary needs to be resurrected, dusted off and separated from its poor bed fellow, mediocre, and given its rightful place as the connecting fabric of the wonderment of the everyday.

A Sense Of Urgency

I am most attached, more so than to my reputation as a counsellor, to a public image of 'teaching well', so it is not a surprise that this 'story' is the last to find a spot on the page even though it has always been a clear contestant for *Bedtime Stories*. It is an obvious example to me of how I am affected, changed and challenged by the work. Yet it was not until Cheryl White gave me an alternative and generous name for my behaviour, a name which helped me to not frighten myself with totalising words of self-criticism, that I have been able to think and write about it more openly.

The phrase Cheryl suggested was 'a sense of urgency' and she helped me to see how this sometimes has me participating in behaviours which disturb me, particularly when I teach. What is different when this sense of urgency highjacks the classroom ambience? I guess if someone was a fly on the wall they might see my teaching style shift from being relatively relaxed, where there was noticeable room for exploration of ideas and a soft eye for changes in group dynamics and humour, to a way of relating which is sharp, tight, and almost dictatorial. Gone is the seemingly endless desire and creative ways to rephrase a question; my usual ability to step back and let the group struggle with a dilemma just vanishes. Enter what I can only presume are obvious accompanying facial changes which reflect my internal conversations of, 'What do you mean, you don't think racism is much of a problem anymore?', or, 'You've never heard of feminism?! We are the same age, for god's sake - where have you been living for the last 40 years?' Outward statements replace questions and, on a really bad day, they become speeches. I want to write that bit really quickly, and defensively add that it doesn't happen very often. But it should never happen that people feel silenced or shut down from learning, or that I use my power in such a situation to support a 'truth' and a single perspective.

When I name this behaviour as a sense of urgency, the grip that shame and embarrassment have on the way I view myself slackens enough for other less critical images to emerge. Only when 'I' am not my sense of urgency can I step away from all the negative things that shame tries to persuade me that I am. Only in this new place of self-reflection is there space for me to begin to reclaim the validity of its intention and purpose, as well as to examine its misdirected ways of operating.

With this naming also comes the lost freedom to swim deeply in the passion that the awareness of a sense of urgency brings to my life; how it strengthens my commitment to not be complacent; how evoking the unshaming component of a sense of urgency assists me to challenge myself and others; how it pushes me to take risks because I cannot assume that the opportunity will come again; and how it encourages me to embrace newness and connection when my old ways of separateness seem the more comfortable option.

Since making the decision that I would include this piece, I have been squinting longsightedly into the world of a sense of urgency, trying to understand its existence in my life. When did this sense of urgency emerge, and in what context am I likely to adopt its ways?

In the travelling of this research/exploration I have found myself drifting back to re-read some of the early feminist writers who have influenced my thinking, women like Audre Lorde and Adrienne Rich, women whose own sense of urgency in fact inspired me to work in the ways that I do now. I had to smile with relief and an inflated sense of being in good company, when I actually read Audre Lorde's description of her reactions as, 'I have a sense of urgency'[4].

Yet it was not in the course of my original reading of these women that I discovered and adopted *their* sense of urgency. More that in their writings I found a language for familiar feelings and unnamed thoughts. Those feelings were/are something like, 'Time is running out and there is so much to do, so much to change; a desperate kind of desire/hope that I need to get everyone on board (my ship?), or at least to not waste time trying to persuade people who are not willing to sail with me'. When I was a child these feelings revolved around a small world, and then grew to fit the habitat of my adult understandings.

Again I return to Cheryl's offered explanation of its possible history, one that I like better than my own essentialist explanations, i.e. 'My *true nature* is authoritarian!' Cheryl commented that this is not an isolated behaviour that she witnesses only in me, but something she says she has seen in lots of women who have been politically active from an early age. I often say that I became a feminist in utero, because even then my twin brother took up more space and I spent most of the time upside down! (He also generously then and now contributed to the development of my consensus and collective ideals since he and I have never known what it is not to share.)

When I return to think about teaching, I wonder: 'Is there *any* situation in which it would be OK for a "sense of urgency" to silence someone's voice? What are my responsibilities as a teacher around learning and promoting conversations of enquiry? Are all conversations equally valid?'

It seems important to loosely make the distinction between the different politics of education. A liberal approach to adult education embraces ideals such as 'equality' meaning giving equal air-space to all ideas, including equal time for the validation of the existing culturally dominant ideas. Another perhaps more feminist approach acknowledges the need to redress the imbalance by actively promoting voices which have been silenced by the dominant voices. It is this latter approach which guides my teaching. Yet the line that this role has me walking is fine and mobile. I do not subscribe to the belief that all voices inherently have equal power to be heard, and yet nor do I want to become the police of conversation.

There is not always confusion. Sometimes my role is clear and the line well lit. For example, when people from the dominant culture interrupt an Aboriginal woman's tutorial presentation to fill in the 'missing historical data' (*her history*), I have no qualms about interrupting those ideas which have people believing that this is appropriate or useful. At other times I walk in the dark chasing an illusive line, crashing unintentionally into a student's confidence.

Yet if it is not always confusing, then what are the criteria upon which I make that distinction? How can I set up a context which makes transparent these differences to others, so this too becomes a part of the conversation, the questioning, the learning? How do I promote space for contradiction, when the temptation is to package the neatness of simplicity?

I do not yet have 'paper' answers, although I have more candles. And I suspect that since I have become more aware of the not-so-useful aspects of a sense of urgency, there have been fewer bruised confidences admitted to casualty and my humour now rarely deserts me. I also have a growing appreciation of just what such a training course demands of people's thinking, how it radically challenges our ways of relating, the ways we see ourselves and our world views.

Despite my desire to review and revise the everyday expression of this sense of urgency, I believe we are living in times when there are strong reasons for a sense of urgency to take centre stage in our thinking. Now, more than ever, is there evidence of global environmental/cultural/physical/emotional and spiritual genocide and I cannot imagine how I could sustain myself without this sense of urgency. And if I had to choose between wearing the consequences of an overactive sense of urgency and trimming its rough edges into the more acceptable shape of damp and diluted enthusiasm, my choice would be clear.

Notes

1. Conversation with Johnella Bird, Co-Director of The Family Therapy Centre, Auckland, New Zealand.
2. Penley-Miller, Kenton, 1994 (unpublished paper): N.H.R.M.C. Suicide Prevention Conference, Canberra, Australia.
3. Conversation with Maxine Joy, Co-Director of Nada, Adelaide, South Australia.
4. Lorde, Audre, 1988: *A Burst of Light*. London: Sheba Feminist Pub.

Acknowledgements

I wish to pay tribute to the following people who have contributed to my thinking and ways of working, and in particular to *Bedtime Stories*.

The people who have consulted with me and given their generous permission for their stories to be told.

Beryl Anderson, my mother, whose love of words and commitment to keeping conversations open spills over me, renewing my hope.

Olympia Kourakis, who believes I can do anything, takes seriously even my wildest dreams, and always finds time for discussion of ideas amid the demands of mothering her two boys, the building of community and paid work.

Pat Ann, whose love and friendship were always strong enough to hold me in the tenuousness of tough and difficult conversations and whose politics consistently challenge my ways of thinking.

Vanessa Swan, who shares my hunger for collaboration, and whose fine mind and willingness to travel blind regularly transports my thinking into new territory.

Dheera Payler, who invited me to appreciate the ordinary through her celebration of the everyday.

Bernadette Roberts, who encourages me to find the balance between the two meanings of 'Leela'.

Rasata Knight, the reclining Buddha, whose courage to walk her own path, inspires me to do the same.

Johnella Bird, who, at the right time and in the right way, reminded me to write first for myself, and to leave the critiquing and the editing for down the track.

Andrea rieniets, who takes the magic of words, throws them deep into her honeyed voice and joins the skies when she lets go, who against the odds has just 'published' her first CD, which inspired me to get Bedtime Stories off the ground.

Cheryl White, the dream-maker, for her unequivocal 'Yes' to the idea of Bedtime Stories and her faith that it would be completed.

Michael White, for his vision, for a way of working that I can finally call home.

Participants in the last 4 years of training courses at Dulwich Centre, who have taught me how to teach.

The Tea-Pot Revolutionaries - Kerry Smith, Alison Topaz, Molly Claire, Mahamarti, Visarjan, Surunga-Rose, Sue Hetzel, Zoy Kazan, and the Dale Street women, for the litres of tea, the passionate arguments, the laughter and the new understandings, which are the gifts of their friendships.

Lisa Berndt

I am fortunate to be part of a community of people - local and international- who are passionate about social justice, and who value humour, collaboration, challenge, playfulness and support.

I work with Bay Area Family Therapy Training Associates in Cuptertino, California, and with Project Respect in San Francisco. Other than this, my dream job would be singing back-up with a rhythm and blues band.

On Remembering What's At Stake
or
'You Get Paid For This?'

A young European-American boy named Thomas and his mother, Adrian, came to my office to discuss how things had been going amongst some recent hard times. While we talked, Thomas played with my stuffed flying pig. He twirled it around and taught it stunts until we were all quite breathless and exhilarated. Thomas stopped abruptly and asked, incredulously, 'You get paid for this?'

What a question! I hadn't asked it in quite a while, even though it was a question which had puzzled me, even troubled me at times. What does it mean to work as a family therapist in Cupertino, California? Where does the pay fit in? What does it mean as a white woman to work against racist oppression and benefit from white supremacy? What does this have to do with therapy? Who do I think I am and how do I get away with it? What do I bring to therapeutic conversations and what do I take? Is it art? Craft? Companionship? Confessional? Fashion? Indulgence?

In the supermarket nearest my San Francisco apartment, there are 183 varieties of breakfast cereal. No kidding. And if you believe the packages (it must be true, it's in print), in at least 90% of them the nutrients were processed right out of the original grains, sacrificed to whatever state of flakiness or pophood or crispness the manufacturers had in mind. It's not food, not exactly, but it's guaranteed not to get soggy in milk. A sad commentary on progress. I always thought: all this technology, all this crunchiness, but where's the nourishment? But wait ... in the bold print, alongside the picture of the action figure to be found inside, the hope: vitamin fortified. What a relief! They figured out how to put food back into the food!

I used to think of psychotherapy this way. The nourishment (community, communion, relationship) is a casualty of progress. Intimacy gets lost, along with fibre and flavour; therapy puts it back. Something about this notion, however, didn't satisfy me. The idea that I could fill and empty *self* left me wondering: with what nutrients and where was my supply and what did I know about corrective additives of emotional experiences? I believed in seeing 'clients' in context, but what about *my* context? What might that say about power relationships? What does it say about any imagined separation between psychotherapy and politics?

When I'm asked what my work means to me, what sustains me in it, I think of the vitality and urgency that comes with seeing the connection of politics and therapy.

When I try to describe that dawning awareness, many scenes come to mind. Here are three of them.

I walk in the hills above town. It is Thanksgiving Day, a holiday with multiple meanings in the US. The pageantry most commonly performed in the dominant culture celebrates the bounty of the land, the survival of 17th century English on North American soil through co-operation with Indigenous people, and the Pilgrims' right to all the land provided. Thanks go to the Pilgrims' God, not to the land or to the people whose lives had been linked to that land for countless generations. It's a kind of holiday of self-congratulation for the Pilgrims' descendants. It's a day for feasting and football, the opening of a holiday season of connecting with friends and family, and preparing for the frenzied consumerism of December.

I look out over the San Francisco Bay to the Golden Gate. Standing small and formidable in the bay is Alcatraz, a small island which houses the shell of a deserted prison. It also holds a history of struggle and resistance of Indigenous peoples. The American Indian Movement came to the attention of the world in the 1970s when a group of Native Americans occupied Alcatraz for several months. They were eventually forced out, but each Thanksgiving Day they host an alternative commemoration at sunrise at Alcatraz. They say 'No' to the consumerism of the season, to the version of history that would render them invisible and justify continued genocide. And they invite all to join them in the affirmation of other values.

I am happy to accept that invitation. Walking in the hills that day, I hear a whisper - from across the bay? from the ground beneath my feet? - 'The earth is bleeding'. I know that it is true, feel some pain, and, somehow, hope. 'That's the good news' the voice assures me, 'It means she's alive'. I walk on. 'Anything else?' I ask. *Remember*, comes the whisper, this time from the trees all around me. There is a solemnity and a smile that comes with the message. 'Remember what?' I asked. *Just remember.*

Another image:

I was on a bus in a tropical region in Nicaragua. The forest was achingly beautiful, with reds and purples and outrageous pinks bursting through the deep wet green that seemed to grow before our eyes. Life in abundance. And death in the air. Three days before, in these hills, a man, his 20-year-old nephew and his 8-year-old niece had been attacked, mutilated and killed by ex-Contra soldiers. The man had been teaching campesinos to read, and was accused of political organising. My horror at the event says much about my sheltered position in the world. The family's friends had seen such occurrences so many times, they knew how to grieve this and all the losses that came before. 'Remember this', they told me, 'and tell about it in your country'.

In my country, I remember, the President of the United States had portrayed such teachers as terrorists and the Contras as freedom fighters, and had supported the Contras financially and politically. I really hadn't given it much thought. What did it have to do with me? Now I had seen the bodies of people who'd risked and lost their lives for work they believed in. I'd met farmers who didn't know if their harvest would carry them through the month, and women who organised neighbourhood kitchens to ensure that the community's children were fed. Global Economics, 101. With the blessing of the World Bank, my country imported beans and rice in such quantities that local farmers could not compete at market, and so could not afford to plant next season, and could not afford to stay on the land. Large companies from overseas could buy the land cheaply, to raise gourmet vegetables for export. Gourmet vegetables.

I thought of the world as I had known it. I grew up in a place and time and community for whom the dominant myths of the culture fitted so well we didn't know they were myths and didn't recognise culture. We were a white, suburban, upper-middle-class, nuclear family: heterosexual couple, two children, two cars (sometimes), assorted pets, house with lawn, parents working at jobs that could pay for their children's advanced education. It was the era of Sputnik, Castro, the Kennedys, The Beatles, Motown, Vietnam, Watts, moon landings, Martin Luther King, Wounded Knee, Kent State, Malcolm X, Attica: but the turmoil and triumphs of the times seemed as (un)real to me as the characters on 'I Dream of Genie' or a Dallas Cowboys' football game. I was protected from knowing. These events had an impact on my family, but it took years to know it. I was shielded from these things. I was shielded from how much they mattered.

Now, in Nicaragua, the mattering was clear and crucial, and I remembered things in a different light. The obfuscations of the past decades, the murders and thefts committed in my name, the minds and lives held hostage to protect my lifestyle. *Remember.*

Another:

A group of us who work together in an anti-violence project in a San Francisco middle-school gather to rejuvenate. We share our reasons for our commitment to undermining institutional racism in the school. I talk about how working in this school with this team reminds me of what's at stake, about how privilege can protect me, a white middle-class woman, from that knowledge. I think, but don't say aloud, how my thoughts are about how to spend each day, not how to survive it. How I can expect a certain degree of institutional protection. How I can worry about the future because I have a good chance of living for a long while. I am fairly fluent in the language of access and I can fake what I don't know.

Then a colleague speaks: as a young African American man, he is aware every time he leaves his house that he may not make it home. That he and his friends cannot gather without being challenged by the police. That he wades daily through layers of fear and prejudice. And that he's gone into social work so that he can be in a position to help young people find their way through this; and that learning the language of academia puts him at risk of losing the friends who have stood by him in the face of the danger, the ones who understand well enough to protect him. He names the strain of translating between worlds every day. What it's like to be afraid, and yet portrayed also as a threat. To be angry, and told he's crazy or inappropriate or overreacting or not patient enough. To have to learn a professional language that inevitably problematises his people.

He speaks from his heart, and the room is filled with the presence of young men who died too soon. 'Too many', says an African American woman through her tears. She's seeing faces I don't see, seeing futures that might have been. I glimpse what the tears might mean, what it might take to live on through them, to go back for the children, even if it means being threatened and insulted and discounted every day. It's a moment of a kind of love and closeness that recognises huge differences, huge injustices; a moment that tells me of my whiteness and how it protects me. *Remember*.

These are moments that come to my mind when I think about what's important for me in my work and my life. They aren't 'therapeutic moments', nor a direct answer to the question. Yet I feel that the answer is glimpsed in these moments, and maybe in the spaces between. I think that therapy and other work for social justice thrive in those spaces, and require us to ask questions about the links between these stories and our own lives.

Remembering. Re-membering, as Michael White suggests. That seems to say something about the work that I do, as a therapist and as an activist, and why I can't imagine separating those roles. How to remember, when I enjoy a privileged position in a system that depends for its survival on forgetting, on dis-membering. What are the languages of remembering? What are the risks of remembering? The costs of forgetting? Is this what privilege means - the option to forget? Is this a definition of power - a monopoly on memory? What are the techniques of forgetting?

I keep thinking that, remembering where we come from, we might walk with more care on the planet. This remembering could be very painful for some of us, since, along with the courage and hard work of our ancestors, we might have to acknowledge the wide and bloody swathe they cut to make room for our present place in the world, in terms of property, privilege, and access to power. It hurts my heart to remember the Chinese, Japanese, and Mexican workers whose labor laid the tracks for the railroad that rewarded my Irish grandfather's work with entry into the middle-class, while their own families were denied not only citizenship, but basic human rights. It hurts to know that my other great-grandfathers, who inherited land granted for killing Indians, organised terrorist raids on Black families and profited from the labour of people kidnapped from Africa. It hurts my heart to see how I have benefited, and continue to benefit, from white supremacy. But the costs of forgetting are high: loneliness, alienation, disorientation, dehumanisation of the forgetters, and continued violation of those who have been wronged. I would rather have my heart hurt than forget that I have one.

Now, I am not talking here about some abreactive experience, some Freudian,

Alfred Hitchcock epiphany where what is repressed is liberated and we all feel better. I'm not even talking about some Jungian connection with a collective unconscious. One of the things I've learned in narrative interviews is that in the remembering are found previously unstoried possibilities for new courses of action. Might there be traditions worth reclaiming? Were there voices for justice? What were the women's experiences? What moral dilemmas did they face? Within what world view, what standard of who counts as human and who does not, did they participate in genocide and consider themselves righteous people? What might this help us see about our current view? Were there gaps in that world view, pockets of resistance?

I've noticed some habits that try to preserve amnesia. Accessories to values such as individualism, competition, survival of the fittest, meritocracy, and the ahistorical even-playing field, can all sabotage this kind of remembering. Some of the most annoying might be blame, shame, scorn, mistrust of others in privileged positions, hoarding of knowledge, ideas of cost-effectiveness, a belief that there is a right way and either it's my way and adopt it, or I will never know it so why bother? The idea that if something is painful or uncomfortable it indicates inadequacy and should be mastered. The list goes on. I don't know if these are artefacts of my culture, of my class, or if they are given power by disciplines of psychology. (Oh - maybe disciplines of psychology *are* artefacts of my culture, and class!) I do know that harsh judgement and practices of individual working through can be paralysing. Ideas like 'I have nothing to give until I get it mastered myself', or, 'I can't love anyone until I love myself', actually play into consumerism's hands by promoting feelings of helplessness and inadequacy among the powerful and developing technologies of amelioration. These ways of thinking co-opt compassion and short-circuit a person's passion for life.

I recently experienced a shock of remembering while watching a film, *Sankofa*. It portrayed the experience of slavery, and in one scene it named a piece of the white experience that had never been articulated to me, one which I recognised in one horrible moment, making sense of all the pieces that had gone before. The scene depicted the moment when the slaves realise that their cruel overseer is alone on the hill, and they take their machetes from the canefields and advance on him. It was the terror of the slaveowner, and of the man whose job it was to protect the fragile system which kept one person the owner and another one the property. It was a terror in which I had been trained extensively and subtly.

This terror wasn't discussed much in the suburbs. I believe my ancestors thought of themselves as a good people, doing what they thought was right within their view of what was moral, within their understanding of who counted as human and who didn't. Dominant philosophies and institutions justified these actions in such a way that highly moral people could commit horrific acts without noticing their impact. Still, what does it say about systems and institutions, and ways of thinking, that they have to be held together by terrorism? What does it say that the terrorism isn't named, and that the oppressed are portrayed as the threat?

The costs of forgetting came together in a way I could no longer ignore when I was in my teens. Maybe it was because I was growing up female in a male-dominated society. Or looking for a clue about love and sex in the face of compulsory heterosexuality. Maybe it was the experience of being a child where reality gets defined by adults. Or maybe, in the 1960s of my childhood, the contradictory images were flooding the airwaves and our consciousnesses faster than old moralities could justify them. The uneasiness I experienced, the silence and the mystification around it, took a shape called dis-ease - *anorexia nervosa* it was called, *dysfunctional family, mother-daughter enmeshment*. My family, friends, and well-meaning doctors, just did not have the language to help me. But on the edges of my 'treatment' among the orderlies and nurses and fellow patients and people I met on the urban streets - many of them from other cultures, other classes - I found sparks of humour and irreverence and frankness and pain and commitment and outrage and mischief. From their positions outside of the dominant culture, they spoke the unspeakable and named the invisible. They gave me hope for alternatives. In my world, they would have been called misfits, lunatics and heretics, and they called me back into life. They offered me hope, another way of being human, a view from the edges of my culture that helped make sense of my experience.

In my work, in my heart, I answer to them. This means keeping hold of that life-line, and extending it when I can. It means honouring a debt that can never be paid. It means taking my place beside these people when I can, and knowing my place when I can't. It means listening for alternative histories, hearing and believing what the voices from the margins of dominant culture are saying, and responding with my heart and with a willingness to follow their lead, to use my privileges as they deem fit. It means keeping in mind that the connection between the family starving in Nicaragua and the young woman starving in the US suburbs suggests other connections. It means that both experiences of privilege and experiences of marginalisation inform how I live and how I work, what I understand and what I can't, where I am welcome and where I am not entitled to enter, much less be trusted. It means standing against injustice inside and outside the therapy room. It means being a guest in people's lives, not a tourist. It means remembering that, as Adrienne Rich says: *When language and naming are power, silence is oppression and violence.*

In narrative therapy I've found a language of exploration and critique, a vocabulary for questions I longed to ask when I was younger. I believe that when therapy allows for the naming of injustice, challenges the discourses that keep oppressive practices in place, and honours practices of resistance and creation of alternatives, it can be part of a revolution in thought. For someone to honour their uneasiness enough to come to therapy can be a gesture of hope and resistance, an act of saying 'No' to the way things have been. In this 'time is money' society, setting aside a period for dialogue and reflection is counter-cultural. It defies individualism and competition to invite other people into the process. I love being included, witnessing acts of courage, participating in the weaving of roots, being invited to a new edge. I see it as a solemn and joyous opportunity to re-member, to learn, to celebrate, and to be a part of a movement.

A friend who has knowledge of botany sees winter not as bleakness and death, but as a time of germinating beneath the surface. The knowledges that people share with me about their lives gives me a similar appreciation, and helps me notice the liveliness, the lilt, the whimsy, the strength in their stories. They keep reminding me: the earth is bleeding, but - it's alive.

So, what does this work mean to me? You mean honestly? A way out, a way in, a way through, a way across - a way to negotiate, with some kind of integrity, the hall of mirrors, the lethargy, the complacency, the rootlessness that protects privilege. A way to keep trying to make sense of things that don't seem to make sense. Reverence for things I wouldn't otherwise have noticed, and irreverence for things I might have held as unchallengeable. Hope. Delight. Ganging up on the executioner. Companionship on the journey. Kinship. Belonging. Re-membering.

So yes, Thomas, I do get paid for this, amply. In more ways than I can express, it's my living.

Acknowledgements

So many people have supported, shared and inspired me in my work -I can't name them all here. Among those who have helped me think about this paper are:

James Shuler	Leanne Black	Linda Kuwatani
Valerie Minor	Shadrach Lipscomb	Toni Foster
Jane Hales	Harold Berlack	Nancy Nagel
Kaern Kraeling	Susan Sandler	Leela Anderson
Joyce Wright	Margy Lim	Nell Myhand
Sharon Gollan	Sharon Martines	Coc Mendoza
Victor Lewis	Amy Epstein	Cheryl White
Zoy Kazan	Daurien Graves	

Janet Adams-Westcott

Janet Adams-Westcott is a psychologist and family therapist who practices in Tulsa, Oklahoma. She provides clinical and administrative supervision at Family & Children Services, Inc.

Challenging Disqualifying Practices

Ginny's Story

When I met Ginny that evening I knew that something was troubling her. She phoned earlier that day asking to be seen prior to her next scheduled appointment. She explained that she was experiencing a return of 'hallucinations' and thoughts of hurting herself.

When she was growing up, Ginny's father told her that she would never amount to anything. For a number of years she believed this story of failure. She began drinking alcohol during her adolescent years and used cocaine heavily in her young adult years. It had been five years since she entered a drug treatment program and taken her life back from chemicals. She became an active participant in support groups, left her abusive partner, entered school, and dedicated herself to helping others escape drug problems. Most of the time, she could challenge her father's story about herself by writing in her journal and having conversations with supportive friends.

When I first met Ginny six months earlier, she had been carrying around a gun and was very concerned she was going to use it to kill herself. In our work together we discovered that Ginny was invited to question her competence and worth as a person in interactions where others acted in disqualifying, intimidating or abusive ways, or when she was exposed to specific sensory cues reminiscent of the sexual abuse she experienced as a child. She was particularly vulnerable to these kinds of thoughts when overtime hours on her job as a nurse in a residential treatment facility interfered with sleeping and connecting with friends.

As she became more exhausted and isolated, Ginny would begin to experience disturbing perceptual experiences that she referred to as 'hallucinations'. As she walked down dark corridors making her rounds on the night shift, she would have the experience of someone watching her from the shadows. She would try to reassure herself that these were just shadows and that she was an adult, not a little girl whose father might come out of the shadows to molest her.

The old story invited Ginny to interpret her perceptual experiences as evidence that she was indeed worthless and would never make it in life. She began to feel more and more out of control as 'the voice' of failure became louder and louder. Temptations to use alcohol or other drugs provided even more evidence she would never amount to anything. Any less than 'perfect' intention, thought or behaviour was added to the story that she was a failure as a person. Taking her life seemed the only escape from the pain of despair and hopelessness that accompanied this view of herself.

Prior to this meeting, my conversations with Ginny had focused on understanding this story of failure. I asked questions that invited her to talk about this story as if it were something separate from herself. We worked together to develop strategies to help her begin to challenge this view of herself. She was beginning to understand why other people might see her as a competent employee and a person of value, and had seen a few glimpses of these qualities in herself. She was most aware of this possibility at work where she had been recently promoted to a supervisory position; however, she considered this possibility to be remote at best. The failure story did not allow her to experience a sense of personal agency so she did not give herself credit for her accomplishments. She attributed her five years of abstinence from chemicals to her 'higher power' and did not see her co-operation with this 'higher power' as having any significance.

I began our conversation that evening by asking Ginny if anything had changed in her life since our meeting the previous week. She explained that she had been experiencing a lot of stress after making a mistake at work. I was curious whether the failure story was inviting her to question her ability to do her job.

When Ginny answered affirmatively, I asked her what had happened to invite the failure story to return. Ginny said that she wasn't sure as she had been careful to stay in touch with friends and avoid working too many hours. I wondered if this idea about failure had taken hold of her before or after she discovered the error at work.

Ginny explained that she had not discovered the error herself, but that it had been brought to her attention by her supervisor. She had always described her supervisor as extremely supportive, so I was curious about what happened when he talked to her about the error. She told me that he commented that it was very unlike her to make mistakes and asked if she was having any problems with her medication.

Given the minor nature of the error, I was curious whether Ginny knew why her supervisor thought there might be some connection between the mistake and the medication she was taking. She explained that it had been just two weeks since he learned she had been hospitalised in the past for 'psychiatric' reasons and continued to take psychotropic medication as prescribed by a psychiatrist.

During a previous session, Ginny told me that many of her colleagues who were 'recovering' believed that people who took medication were continuing their addiction. When I asked her what she thought about taking medication, she told me that most of the time she believed that taking the medication was in her best interest. During times when the failure story took over, she began to doubt her own judgment, wonder if her colleagues were right, and view the medication as one more example of her failure in life.

I wondered how Ginny thought her supervisor reacted to this new information about her past. She told me that he was quite surprised and told her that he had never thought of her as a 'dual'. She explained to me that a 'dual' was someone who had a history of both drug problems and a mental health diagnosis. I asked her to tell me about her supervisor's ideas about people who were described by the label 'dual'. I was curious how he thought people who were overcoming both types of problem were different from those who were just 'recovering from addictions'.

She explained to me that the primary difference had to do with 'prognosis'. 'Recovering' people were capable of a 'high level of functioning' as long as they worked their 12-step program. People with chemical dependency and mental health problems were often 'unstable' and had to be closely monitored to prevent them from 'decompensating'.

I wondered if Ginny had ever worked with someone who had been given the label 'dual'. I was curious how this monitoring affected people: Did it make a difference to how they saw themselves? Did it affect their experience of competence and self-worth? How were they affected by the expectation that they were likely to 'decompensate'?

Ginny suggested that people who saw themselves as 'duals' would have difficulty trusting themselves, given that other people were always watching them for evidence of instability. They would be likely to monitor their own behaviour and be oversensitive to any signs they were decompensating. The constant possibility of relapse might prevent them from believing in their own abilities.

I commented that it sounded to me like they might have the experience of being treated as a label or a stereotype instead of as a person. Ginny thought they probably felt this way. I asked if she had ever worked with someone who had encountered some kind of subtle prejudice. I was curious how she worked with the person to help him/her overcome the negative effects of such discrimination. What ideas did they come up with that helped the person turn down invitations from family, friends or professionals to picture himself or herself like a stereotype instead of a unique individual?

Ginny began to talk about her own experiences. She realised that she began to see herself as a 'dual' after the conversation with her supervisor. She believed that, in the past, he might have explained her error as 'just being human'. His question about her medication invited her to believe that he was looking for signs of decompensation. The failure story re-emerged as she began to think of herself as a 'dual' and monitor her own feelings, thoughts and behaviour. The return of 'hallucinations' and suicidal thoughts confirmed the diagnosis and poor prognosis.

I wondered if any of the ideas Ginny came up with while working with her 'patients' might help her turn down invitations to see herself as a 'dual'. I was also interested in her ideas about how experiencing this kind of discrimination influenced the failure story.

Ginny decided that it would be helpful to remind herself that 'dual' was 'just a label'. She believed that she would feel more competent if she quit watching herself for evidence of instability. She thought that she could turn down invitations from other people to feel and act like a 'dual' by recognising their attitudes and behaviour as a form of prejudice. She thought that she could challenge these biases by trusting her own judgement and her ability to do her job. She believed that having this experience could help her overcome the influence of this prejudice in her work with others.

Reflections on the Past Journey

After Ginny left my office that evening, I was struck by the poignant way in which our conversation illustrated the potential for professional knowledges to be used to objectify people and disqualify their experiences. As I drove home, I realised that the disqualification that seemed so compelling that night would not always have been so visible to me.

As therapists in training, we are taught a variety of practices that create 'professional distance' between ourselves and the people we serve. We learn to translate the words people use to describe their experience into psychiatric language. We use this language to create 'confidential' documents such as case notes and psychological evaluations that can be reviewed only by professional audiences. These documents are used to categorise people according to diagnostic labels (Bird 1994; White 1995).

The distance created by these practices makes us vulnerable to seeing those who seek our services as 'cases' rather than people (Carpenter 1994). We may inadvertently invite people to behave in ways that are consistent with the labels we have assigned them. Over time, people begin to internalise these pathologised descriptions of themselves and invite others to see them in this way.

Today, I strive to be ever-vigilant to the possibility that I might inadvertently engage in practices that have the effect of disqualifying the people they were intended to assist. This journey is an ongoing one and has involved countless discoveries along the way.

Searching for Truth and Expertise

I did my professional training in psychology and was taught to use the scientific method to seek 'empirical truth'. I was taught to privilege data over experience, conduct evaluations to measure 'intelligence' and 'personality', and write reports about test scores rather than people. If I had met Ginny during these formative years, I would not have driven home after our session, but would have gone directly to the library to begin reviewing the professional literature on dual diagnosis.

I would have been interested in translating Ginny's descriptions of her experiences into psychiatric language. In Ginny's 'case', the translation would have been facilitated by her knowledge of professional jargon. Her use of the words 'hallucinations' and 'voices' would have invited me to conclude that Ginny suffered from a psychotic or bipolar disorder.

This diagnosis would have strongly influenced my expectations for an interaction with Ginny. I would have shared her supervisor's view that the prognosis was 'guarded' and that she was extremely vulnerable to relapse. Rather than drawing on her personal and professional experience in the treatment of drug problems, I would have expected myself to take an expert stance and use the literature to formulate a treatment plan. Most likely, the goals I developed would not involve change, but would focus on helping her 'maintain her current level of functioning'. This approach might have had the effect of reinforcing her difficulty in trusting her own experiences, and inviting her to see herself and interact with others as if she were a 'dual'.

Experiencing the Power of 'the Gaze'

My first discovery of the potential for professional knowledges to disqualify was intensely personal. Though I expected myself to take an expert stance in my work with 'clients', I was never comfortable with this role. Early in my training I attributed my discomfort with power and certainty to my youth and inexperience. (I remember hoping for some strands of grey hair and a few wrinkles.)

Supervisors commented on my ease in joining with clients and mastery of various techniques, but questioned why I was so 'tentative' in introducing ideas or directing sessions. I was invited to discover where this 'tentativeness' came from by 'doing work with my family-of-origin'. As my discomfort became defined as a problem, I became more and more immobilised in situations where other professionals observed my work. My search for answers in family of origin work orientated me to deficits, and I began to pathologise myself as a person and question my work as a therapist.

I began to make sense out of these experiences some years later when I read a description by Michael White (1989) of Foucault's analysis of the specifying effects of surveillance practices. White writes about the way in which people who are subject to the evaluative 'gaze' of others begin to disqualify themselves by constantly observing their own experiences to see if they measure up to particular standards. In much the same way as Ginny began to evaluate herself according to her supervisor's expectations of 'duals', I began to evaluate myself according to my interpretation of my supervisor's ideas about how therapists demonstrated their expertise.

Learning to Privilege Experience

A major transformation in my experience of both the people I work with and myself as a therapist occurred when I was assigned to provide outreach services in several rural communities. At the time, there was little written on home-based therapy. Without 'the literature' to guide me, I found myself relying on my own experiences as a person and a professional. Away from the watchful eyes of my supervisors, I easily took an active role in sessions without coming from a position of expertise.

I also came to rely much more on the experiences of the people with whom I worked. The 'professional distance' that seemed so important in the office seemed much less meaningful when I was an invited guest in people's homes. It was no longer possible for me to objectify people and see them as 'cases'. I witnessed first hand the adversity faced by these families and quickly developed an extreme respect for their abilities. They taught me the importance of co-creating change and developing partnerships with the large community.

Adopting a Collaborative Stance

It wasn't until my first experience as a supervisor that I finally quit disqualifying myself for my discomfort with the expert role. I spent a year learning the Milan model and found the idea that hypotheses are more or less useful, particularly liberating. I began to replace the quest for certainty with curiosity and a consideration of 'fit'. Rather than advocating one correct view, I asked questions that invited students to consider multiple perspectives by juxtaposing various therapy models and considering which interventions 'fitted' for the people they were working with and for themselves in their current development as therapists.

As I discussed the notion of 'fit' with students, it finally became clear to me that my struggle with taking an expert stance had always been an issue of lack of fit. My preference for a collaborative stance was validated when I discovered the narrative approaches of Michael White (1986), Tom Anderson (1987), and Harlene Anderson and Harry Goolishian (1988).

Challenging Restraints Instead of Resistance

I became more aware of the potentially disqualifying effects of our professional practices when I began to work in a treatment program for families with children who had experienced child sexual abuse. At the time, several members of the therapy team were questioning traditional ideas that viewed the families they worked with as extremely dysfunctional and highly resistant to change. They experienced their work 'confronting denial and psychopathology' as adversarial and extremely exhausting. They felt responsible for insuring the continued safety of child victims, and struggled with balancing what they perceived as their dual roles of psychotherapist and social control agent. They were attracted to family systems ideas, but agreed with feminist critiques about the failure of the field to adequately address issues of power (cf. Flaskas & Humphreys 1993 for a review).

After being introduced to the work of Michael White (1986; White & Tomm 1987), we began to experience the families we worked with as 'restrained' rather than 'resistant'. Instead of locating the problem inside a person or in relationships between people, we began to locate the problem in those restraining beliefs, patterns of interactions, and cultural expectations and practices that created vulnerability to abuse for that particular family (Adams-Westcott, Dafford & Sterne 1993; Adams-Westcott & Isenbart 1990). We began to ask questions to invite family members to think about these beliefs and behaviours as separate from or external to themselves.

We were immediately struck by the positive effects of this new perspective. By considering cultural expectations and practices, this new way of thinking allowed us to address issues of power in a way that invited accountability. Perceiving the problem as something outside of themselves invited family members to begin to experience themselves in new ways. The adults recognised, often for the first time, that they could choose to continue co-operation with the restraints or assume personal responsibility for challenging abuse and its effects. Those parents who had perpetrated abuse began to acknowledge the devastating effects of their behaviour on their children and hold themselves accountable for ensuring the safety of their family members and community. The children we worked with began to understand that, although they had been victimised, they did not have to adopt a victim story. We invited them to develop stories about themselves that highlighted the courage and strength they demonstrated by escaping secrecy and challenging the effects of abuse.

We were also struck by the liberating effects of this approach on our experiences of ourselves as therapists. As the parents we worked with assumed more responsibility for their behaviour, we realised that we had been restrained by the level of responsibility we felt we needed to take to prevent future abuse. As the focus of our work shifted from confronting denial and psychopathology to highlighting strengths and progress, we began to access our own resources as people and as therapists. We experienced a new sense of generativity as we began to think of our role as collaborating with family members to co-create change.

Discovering the Power of Stories

It was in this context that I observed the power of stories to facilitate or impede change. For example, non-offending parents who did not immediately believe their children at the time the abuse was revealed were often labelled as 'unfit mothers' by the members of the larger system. Reports of their progress towards treatment goals were often disqualified by those professionals who interacted with them at the time of disclosure. These professionals sometimes questioned the authenticity of changes made by the parents. At other times, they questioned the soundness of our approach, or our competence and objectivity as therapists.

Differences with other professionals sometimes led to a battle of the 'experts' in the courtroom. We were most tempted to use our power as professionals to create certainty when we feared that young children might go home to parents who we believed had not taken responsibility for changing their abusive behaviour. Team members often disagreed about the limits of our role and expertise in these circumstances, and were vulnerable to participating in disqualifying practices with each other (see Jenkins 1994 for a discussion of issues of power and politics in working with abuse).

The challenges we received from other professionals had the effect of inviting us to question our work and revisit more traditional stories about therapy. On these 'visits' we discovered that, even when we tried, we were no longer able to see the people we worked with as the problem. Some team members decided to leave the sexual abuse treatment program and continued to use narrative ideas with people presenting with problems where the consequences of 'relapse' were less devastating. Other people continued to work on the team, but turned their attention to other approaches. A few of us began to share our work using narrative ideas with other therapists who were also questioning traditional ideas. These conversations were extremely affirming and encouraged us to continue our work.

Creating an Audience for Evolving Stories

Our own experiences adopting this new story about therapy influenced us to begin to think of change as a rite of passage (Adams-Westcott & Isenbart 1990; Koback & Waters 1984; White & Epston 1990). Our evolution included a separation from an old way of thinking that no longer fitted for us as therapists, an exploration of new ideas and practices, and an incorporation of more preferred ways of working. The validating conversations we had with colleagues convinced us of the importance of recruiting an audience to help people internalise more preferred stories about themselves.

Instead of assuming the families we worked with were 'stuck', we began to assume that disclosure occurred because family members had already begun to separate from restraining stories. A group treatment approach was developed to create a community to validate and celebrate the steps participants had already taken to escape abuse. The group meetings provided a context for people to experiment with new beliefs and behaviours. Interacting with group members in a more preferred way created lived experiences that reinforced the evolving story (see Adams-Westcott & Isenbart 1995 for a more detailed discussion of the use of group therapy to help people incorporate more preferred stories).

Family members began to invite professionals from the larger systems to individual and family sessions to catch them up with their ongoing progress. Through this process, members of the larger system served as an audience to the developing stories.

Consultants became a vital part of the program (Epston & White 1990). Non-offending parents and children were invited to serve as consultants to provide hope for people newer to the process of change. Men who were nearing the end of treatment for perpetrating abuse served as co-therapists to invite participants in groups for men who were just beginning therapy to assume responsibility for their behaviour. Sharing their own stories helped these consultants internalise more preferred ways of thinking and interacting.

Consultants also helped to hold us accountable by providing feedback about the positive and negative effects of our practices as therapists (McLean 1994; White 1995). This feedback was often painful, and we were tempted to fall back into the practice of pathologising the person rather than giving his or her view serious consideration. We sought to resist this temptation by inviting each other to consider the effects of engaging in these practices on the person providing the feedback and on ourselves.

Taking a Political Stance

Our conversations with people who sought our services made us more acutely aware of the ways in which patriarchal values, prevalent in the larger culture, contribute to the development and maintenance of abuse. We were invited to examine our assumptions and practices by feminist writers (cf. Goodrich 1991) who argued that most therapy models were developed within a cultural context that privileged male dominance and, as a result, inadvertently perpetuated gender inequality.

We struggled with developing interventions that challenged these ideas without disqualifying the people who held them. We were inspired by the work of Alan Jenkins (1990), and began to ask the people we worked with questions about the fit between cultural beliefs about gender roles and expectations and their own preferences about how they want to be as men and women. This helped them begin to discover the extent to which they were oppressed by cultural practices and to take responsibility for challenging them in their everyday lives.

Reflections on the Journey in the Present

My awareness of the potentially disqualifying effects of many of our professional practices has invited me to assume increasing responsibility for challenging these practices in my roles as a therapist, supervisor, teacher and administrator. Despite my commitment to developing more validating ways of working, I am continuing to uncover subtle ways that I co-operate with disqualification.

One of my biggest challenges has been to avoid imposing my enthusiasm for narrative approaches on the people I supervise. If I am not ever-vigilant to issues of power, I run the risk of colonising my perspective or disqualifying those who embrace other perspectives (Amundson, Steward, & Valentine 1993; Kazan 1994; White 1995). I have discovered that this risk is highest with people who are enthusiastic about perspectives I experience as pathologising.

As an administrator, I continue to be challenged by working within a health care system where standards of practice and reimbursement are based on models of psychopathology. My colleagues and I face a continual struggle with how to develop practices that are accountable to accreditors and payors without disqualifying the people who seek our services.

My greatest challenge in my role as a manager is minimising the potentially negative influences of business practices based on patriarchal notions of power and hierarchy. I have found it necessary to interact from a position of expertise in certain situations, particularly those situations that involve professional and legal liability. My colleagues and I are always having conversations about ways we can exert influence while respecting the position and expertise of the other.

The lessons from the past have helped me adopt practices to resist disqualifying practices and interact in more validating ways. I have found it helpful to make disqualifying practices more visible by describing them in externalised language. These descriptions help me to understand how I get recruited into participating in such practices and to suggest potential counter-practices.

To this end, I have been influenced by Ken Stewart's (1991) discussion of the ways in which power is used in relationships. Externalising what he describes as an 'overpowering stance' has helped me turn down invitations to use language to create certainty and impose my ideas on others. I prefer to interact from what Stewart describes as an 'empowered stance'. This way of relating is characterised by genuine curiosity about the ideas of others, a respect for their competencies and unique knowledges and collaboration in developing solutions.

In my experience, more validating practices are invited by an awareness of multiple perspectives. I continue to invite myself and other people to juxtapose different views. I continue to ask questions about which perspective 'fits' for the person. I am also curious about the 'real effects' of each perspective. I ask questions about how each story impacts on the person I am talking with and the people with whom he or she is interacting. Today, I am more likely to be transparent about my own beliefs and to share what 'fits' for me as one of many alternative perspectives.

Reflections on Future Journeys

Given that professional knowledges have become incorporated into the larger culture, increasing awareness of disqualifying practices seems critical to helping people like Ginny overcome the effects of such practices. The following questions were developed to help identify and challenge disqualifying practices:

- What story (or stories) am I telling myself about the person with whom I'm in conversation? How does this story privilege the person's lived experience?
- What are the real effects of the problem on the person?
- Am I using language that locates the problem outside of the person?
- What invitations have I turned down to translate the person's experience into

psychiatric language? What invitations have I turned down to pathologise the person?

- Am I asking questions from a stance of curiosity or a position of certainty?
- What questions can I ask to invite the person to develop self-knowledge and become an expert on him/herself?
- What questions can I ask to invite the person to consider the fit between certain beliefs and practices and his or her preferred beliefs and practices?
- How have I invited the person to consider alternative stories that include the experience of personal agency?
- Is there a way to recruit significant people to serve as an audience to help the person celebrate change and incorporate a new story about him/herself?
- Have I considered the ways in which inequities of gender, race, class, age or sexual orientation may be influencing the person?
- What are the real effects of my practices on the person? What are the real effects of my power as a professional?
- What power tactics am I most vulnerable to participating in? How have I turned down invitations to impose this power on the person?
- How can I share my knowledge and experiences in a way that privileges the knowledge and experience of the person?
- What egalitarian practices have I adopted to minimise the power differential between myself and the people with whom I work?
- Have I shared the ideas or experiences that led me to ask particular questions?
- How have I invited the people I work with to give me ongoing feedback about the positive and negative effects of our work together?
- How can I communicate with people who ascribe to psychiatric stories in a way that maintains my integrity and credibility and does not disqualify the person?

My understanding of disqualifying practices continues to evolve. Asking these kinds of questions has invited me to examine some difficult issues. Like any rite of passage, the work has been both disconcerting and rewarding. I have been encouraged by my experiences helping people like Ginny challenge the effects of professional disqualification. I have celebrated the ways in which students have experimented with diverse ideas and made them their own. I have developed a framework to exercise my power as an administrator and manager to create partnerships and, when necessary, to take an expert stance without invalidating others. It is my hope that continuing to examine these issues will help me and the people I work with to incorporate more validating practices into our professional and personal lives.

References

Adams-Westcott, J., Dafford, T. & Sterne, P. 1993:
'Escaping victim life stories and co-creating personal agency.' In Gilligan, S. & Price, R. (eds), *Therapeutic Conversations.* New York: W W Norton.

Adams-Westcott, J. & Isenbart, D. 1995:
'A journey of change through connection.' In Friedman, S. (ed), *The Reflecting Team in Action. Collaborative practice in family therapy.* New York: Guilford Press.

Adams-Westcott, J. & Isenbart, D. 1990:
'Using rituals to empower family members who have experienced child sexual abuse.' In Durrant, M. & White, C. (eds), *Ideas for Therapy with Sexual Abuse.* Adelaide, South Australia: Dulwich Centre Publications.

Amundson, J., Steward, K. & Valentine, L. 1993:
'Temptations of power and certainty.' *Journal of Marital and Family Therapy,* 19:111-123.

Anderson, T. 1987:
'The reflecting team. Dialogue and meta-dialogue in clinical work.' *Family Process,* 26:415-428.

Anderson, H. & Goolishian, H. 1988:
'Human systems as linguistic systems: Preliminary and evolving ideas about the implications of clinical theory.' *Family Process,* 27:371-394.

Bird, J. 1994:
'Talking amongst ourselves.' *Dulwich Centre Newsletter,* 1:44-46.

Carpenter, J. 1994:
'Finding people in family therapy.' *Dulwich Centre Newsletter,* 1:32-38.

Epston, D. & White, M. 1989:
'Consulting your consultants: The documentation of alternative knowledges.' *Dulwich Centre Newsletter,* 4:25-35.

Flaskas, C. & Humphreys, C. 1993:
'Theorising about power: Intersecting the ideas of Foucault with the "problem" of power in family therapy.' *Family Process,* 32:35-47.

Goodrich, T. (ed) 1991:
Women and Power: Perspectives for family therapy. New York: W.W.Norton.

Jenkins, A. 1990:
Invitations to Responsibility: The therapeutic engagement of men who are violent and abusive. Adelaide, South Australia: Dulwich Centre Publications.

Jenkins, A. 1994:
'Therapy for abuse or therapy as abuse?' *Dulwich Centre Newsletter,* 1:11-19.

Kazan, Z. 1994:
'Power: A multi-dimensional perspective.' *Dulwich Centre Newsletter,* 1:28-31.

Koback, R. & Waters, D. 1984:
'Family therapy as a rite of passage: Play's the thing.' *Family Process,* 23:89-100.

McLean, C. 1994:
'A conversation about accountability with Michael White.' *Dulwich Centre Newsletter,* 2&3.

Stewart, K. 1991:
'Three stances on a theme of power, certainty and intimacy.' *Dulwich Centre Newsletter,* 2.

White, M. 1986:
'Negative explanation, restraint & double description: A template for family therapy.' *Family Process,* 25:169-184.

White, M. 1988:
    'The externalizing of the problem.' *Dulwich Centre Newsletter*, 3-21.
White, M. 1995:
    Re-authoring Lives: Interviews & essays. Adelaide, South Australia: Dulwich Centre Publications.
White, M. & Epston, D. 1990:
    Narrative Means to Therapeutic Ends. New York: W.W.Norton.
White, M. & Tomm, K. 1987:
    'Externalising the problem.' Workshop presentation, Tulsa. Oklahoma.

Acknowledgements

Acknowledgement is extended to all those people who have sought my professional services and allowed me to be part of their journey. I appreciate all the lessons they have taught me and the many ways they have enriched my life.

A special acknowledgement is extended to Ginny for allowing me to share her story so that others might learn from her courage and determination in challenging disqualifying practices.

I want to express my appreciation to current and former colleagues at Family & Children's Services who accompanied me on this journey: Claudia Arthrell, Randy Feller, Deanna Isenbart, Gail Lapidus, Lyn Lucas, Sidney Nelson-Hunt, Beth Persac, DeeDee Smith, Pat Sterne and Yolanda Walker.

I also want to acknowledge the contribution of Jeff Zimmerman, for his special skill in helping students and colleagues find their own direction.

Alison Topaz

I am a Lesbian, a Feminist, a Mother, a Nurse ...

I write as a way to unravel these labels and to ruffle some of the neatness they can pretend.

I have worked in women's health services for the past eight years and am currently in a Women's Health Centre in South Australia. I continue to be nourished by the extraordinary sharing of intimacy, hardship, joy ... that occurs often in visiting women's lives through my work.

I live with my daughter who questions and discovers many things and shares my tendencies for tacky television, late nights and take-away food.

I am attracted to conversation and ideas and being amongst people; particularly women, most often lesbians.

It feels slightly embarrassing to confirm that parts of 'No Pockets' are indeed autobiographical.

No Pockets

Eleanor quite looks forward to a beer or two on a Friday night. Not perhaps every Friday, and often more than two. There's a couple of places she could go, and she fancies herself flexible and not predictable. It's just that there's really only one lesbian bar in town.

Eleanor likes the company of lesbians and would quite favour a new love interest. She can play 8-ball with some reliability and finds conversation possible with strangers. Eleanor has new boots.

The bar is small and narrow and choked with thick smoke that seems to have captured women in islands about the room. She scans for familiar land-marks and sets out. Eleanor likes the thrill of being out alone and savours the uncertainty of the next conversation. She feels known and anonymous here and can travel lightly. She carries her money and single housekey in her left boot as she is dressed without pockets, no place for business cards of duty.

Last week Eleanor went out with pockets and was contemplating her first drink when a woman fell to her feet with a thud. Taking this in, Eleanor decided on closer inspection. She checked pulse, breathing, consciousness, looked for signs of injury and noted the absence of Medic-alert jewellery. She loosened clothing, remembered the coma position, all the while talking, soothing, warding off onlookers and directing someone to call an ambulance. 'Trust me, I'm a nurse.' With a card in her pocket and sensible shoes. She doesn't work in a hospital and really couldn't remember how to give an injection or tie a sling. She knows about smear tests and heterosexual dominance and the politics of menopause. She wonders if she'll always be a nurse in the same way that people say, 'You'll always be a mother, even when your daughter is seventy two'.

Eleanor talks and laughs, navigates some new acquaintanceships and gets swept up for a dance with a friend. She manages a few tricky shots on the pool table and makes a date with an ex-lover for lunch. She burrows in her boot for a beer now and then, but can't dislodge the gold coin between her toes.

Eleanor suspects she's really a counsellor too, by day, and seeks to leave that card at home on Friday nights as well. But here, even in her new boots and no pockets, she finds herself battling with the appropriate response to ... 'my girlfriend-won't-let-me-go-out-alone-and-holds-the-sole-cheque-book-to-our-joint-account'. Eleanor makes brief and deep eye contact with a woman who wept with despair and joy when telling her coming out story at last Thursday's appointment - she'd made time to attend to 'when we meet beyond this room', and wonders if it now seems clumsy to the woman as well. Finding the bathroom, Eleanor ponders how Brenda the plumber might respond to a dripping tap at Mardi Gras. Eleanor knows about Confidentiality and Duty of Care and the Nurses' Code of Conduct. She pays her union fees and wonders how many lesbians *really* use dams.

Stopping for a moment on the edge of the dance floor, Eleanor adjusts her eyes to the dimness and smoke. She feels waves of attention on her and on her new boots, and wriggles her toes with a smile. It's a good night with new boots and travelling lightly; she glances down with this thought. With horror she sees a trail of toilet paper billowing from the bathroom to its anchor at the tip of her boot. For a long second she stands very still. Then, with her eyes slowly searching for familiar sights, she shakes free her foot and shrugs off a blush. She feels known and anonymous here and doesn't much mind if she doesn't find a love interest tonight. She laughs at herself and sails through the room, for there's *only one way out.*

Judith Myers-Avis

Judith Myers-Avis is a feminist therapist and educator who teaches couple and family therapy at the University of Guelph in Ontario, Canada. She is particularly interested in integrating feminist and narrative ideas to help people free their lives from abuse and oppression. She is also a learner and explorer whose journey continues to unfold in unexpected and wonderful ways.

Parallel Journeys

As I reflect on the question of how my work affects my life, I realise that this is not a uni-directional process. To fully capture its three-dimensionality and recursiveness, I must also reflect on how my life affects my work. In the time since I was invited to write this paper, I have contemplated these questions with each therapeutic conversation, and, with my consciousness thus attuned, I have become increasingly aware of the complex interactions between my clients' stories and my own. I can fairly say that my life and being are touched in some way by every client's journey and by every therapeutic conversation - some in whisper-soft ways, some profoundly. And I can also say that, as my own journey has deepened and expanded, my ability to be fully present with each client and to hear the pain, the joy, the possibilities, the fears, the courage, and the nuances of hope and nobility in their story, has deepened and grown beyond what I would earlier have believed possible. I have come to believe that I can go with clients only as far as I have been able to go myself - that where my own process is blocked, so, too, is my ability to be fully available and effective in working with clients in those areas.

In this paper, I will develop these two threads - how my life has been profoundly enriched by the privilege of talking with people about their lives, and how my therapeutic work has been profoundly enriched by my own processes of growth and learning. It is difficult to decide with which side of this interactive process to begin, since each feeds and nourishes the other, and any particular starting point is necessarily arbitrary. For the sake of simplicity, I will begin with some reflections about how others' journeys, shared in the therapy hour, have affected mine.

One of the most significant ways in which my work with clients has impacted on my life has been in the expansion of my understanding of the heights and depths of which human beings are capable. As I have worked with men and women who experienced severe emotional, physical and sexual abuse as children, I have been deeply affected by both the intensity of their pain and the joy of their healing. Witnessing the courage of these persons as they have taken their lives back from the ravages of abuse has touched me at the core of my being. It has taught me about the resilience of the human spirit and its ability to overcome even the most horrific and devastating of experiences. This knowledge has inspired and sustained me, reminding me that if others have been able to overcome the intolerable, then I can find the courage to deal with the lesser abuses in my own life.

Bearing witness to these clients' stories has also challenged my naiveté, and forced me to expand my understanding of the pain human beings are capable of inflicting upon one another. This knowledge has been difficult to accept, puncturing as it has my illusion of safety and rather simplistic belief in innate human goodness. It has forced me to incorporate ideas about the human potential for destructiveness, cruelty and evil, and, in so doing, has intensified my commitment to nurture constructive, healing relationships. Work with these courageous clients has also brought hitherto unexamined aspects of my own life into focus, forcing me to acknowledge and name both the pain I have experienced and that which I have inflicted.

A wonderful and amazing gift from my conversations with clients has been the recurring experience of becoming aware of an issue in my own life, and almost immediately having a client begin talking about a similar issue in theirs. I have been startled, for example, to become aware of the need for greater balance in my life, and soon thereafter to have a client begin her session by announcing that what she needs to talk about today is finding greater balance. Or to become concerned about ways in which I might be giving myself away in a relationship, only to have a client raise a similar question. When I first became conscious of this phenomenon, I wondered if I wasn't, in some way, subtly directing the conversation in a particular direction. However, try as I might to identify ways in which I might be influencing the focus, I cannot uncover the process. This has happened in relation to so many issues in my life: recognising how criticism and anger may contaminate relationships with those I love; coping with separation, divorce, living alone, loneliness; coping with feelings of vulnerability and loss following physical injury; experiencing the death of a parent; struggling to find the fine balance of letting adult children go while remaining supportive and available; taking my life back from the tyranny of perfectionism; finding courage to use my voice, and living with the consequences of doing so; claiming agency in my life; finding meaning.

I am puzzled by the frequency of seeing my own issues reflected in my client's lives, and by the apparent spontaneity of this occurrence. Perhaps I am simply more, or differently, attuned to issues clients raise when I have identified them in my own life. Or perhaps they are such universal issues that some client is bound to raise them at some point while I am focusing on them myself. Perhaps. But that really does not quite fit my experience. Whatever the 'truth' of it, I prefer to regard this phenomenon as a priceless gift from the people who share their lives with me - a mirror which enables me to see my own life issues more clearly and to hear the complexities and nuances of dealing with them more fully. This mirror also functions retroactively. When clients raise issues with which I have already dealt, even many years earlier, I am able to revisit my own past experience, often gaining new insights, appreciation of meanings, and compassion for my younger self.

There is also the complex interplay of my responses to clients' stories and the impact of my responses, in turn, on me. As I listen to clients' stories, I am able to hear clearly their courage, their history of protest, their nobility, and the complicated web of feelings and intentions and desires and beliefs that shape the telling - so much more clearly than I can hear or see them in my own story. I hear my words as I point out all the ways in which a woman has protested against oppression in her life, including childhood tantrums when she was about to be left with a sexually abusive baby-sitter, and I become more conscious of the history of protest in my own life. I listen to myself saying to another woman that the most important relationship she has is the one with herself, and I am reminded of the centrality of my relationship with *my*self. As I observe another client's innate wisdom about his own life and another's courage in confronting fear, I recognise my own wisdom and courage. All of these strengths of the human spirit, which are so much easier to recognise in others, become more evident to me in my own life as I listen to and talk with clients.

My conversations with clients have taught me deeply about life. They have given me a new understanding of the essence of the human condition, of the universal and immutable aspects of life, including loss, pain, illness, and death, as well as birth, growth, love, compassion, kindness, trust, loyalty, and courage. They have enabled me to begin to comprehend the great paradox: that we must make peace with the knowledge that we do not have ultimate control over our lives, while at the same time exercising responsibility and choice in those areas where we do have control. And they have taught me the healing power of laughter in those poignant moments when we recognise our foibles and acknowledge our humanness.

Quite simply, my clients inspire and motivate me. As I work with a man with no memories of his childhood except his abuse of another child, who is largely cut off from intimate connection with himself and his emotions, I am moved by his determination to take his life back from fear and drivenness, and by his committed work to reclaim the fullness of his being. As a woman shares her terror that her anger and criticism may drive her partner away and poison their relationship, I am inspired by her honesty and willingness to be vulnerable in confronting these issues in her life. As a couple challenge emotional abuse and anger in their relationship, I am moved and given hope as I witness their commitment to each other and to reclaiming their relationship from the effects of the childhood abuse each has suffered. These courageous people and their journeys, their dignity, integrity, and wisdom, their determination, commitment, resilience, and faith, their refusal to succumb to despair, their willingness to reach deep within to find the courage to persevere, to make their lives their own, to care deeply for themselves and others, and to overcome the ravages of injustice and oppression - all these have been gifts beyond measure, reminding me of what is possible for the human spirit. Often, when people hear I am a therapist, they comment about how depressing this work must be and wonder how I manage not to become overwhelmed or exhausted. This comment never ceases to amaze me in its distance from the truth. To work with people in the unfolding journeys of their lives is to work daily in the realm of inspiration and hope. It is to witness the small acts of courage and love which remind me constantly of what is possible and of what is truly important.

As I reflect on the intricacies of this dance between clients' journeys and my own, I can also see that the flow and pattern of my own life consistently shape the direction and depth of my work. As I consider the multiple threads of my personal journey over the 29 years since I first began talking with clients, I am struck, as I am sure many seasoned therapists must be, by what I have learned not only about therapeutic processes, but about life itself. It may be self-evident that there cannot be much comparison between the work of a 22-year-old neophyte therapist, with little experience of life, who thought she knew a great deal, and that of a 51-year-old veteran, well-tempered in the crucible of life and all too aware of how little she really knows. Yet, as I look back on my life as a therapist, I see a repeated pattern which stands out beyond merely living more years or learning more about therapy - that is, the impact on my therapeutic work of the work I have done on my own life issues. Again and again it is clear that I can only accompany clients as far as I have gone myself, that I work differently with clients once I have faced my own challenges and confronted my own pain. That if I have not recognised oppression in my own life, I am not likely to recognise it readily in theirs. That if I have not heard myself, I am less likely to really hear them. That if I have not developed empathy and compassion for myself, I am less likely to have them for clients. That if I have not escaped from self-judgement, I am less likely to recognise its strangle-hold on others.

This phenomenon can be seen, of course, in many life situations where we commonly observe that we did not fully understand something until we experienced it ourselves: the frustrations (as well as the joys) of parenthood; the self-judgement involved in struggling with an acting-out adolescent; the sadness and self-questioning that accompanies an ended marriage; the grief of a parent's death; the incomparable loss of a child's death. I don't wish to imply that I think we can only work effectively with those people whose experience duplicates our own, but rather that our understanding deepens and expands with the intimate knowledge of direct experience. Thus my father's recent death taught me, as nothing else had, the unique significance of a parent's death. My empathy for those experiencing this loss changed as I understood more fully the possible complexity of meanings of this life passage. In addition, my ability to understand others' experiences may be expanded through recognition of similar but different threads in my own. My understanding of the desperation of the suicidal client thus grows through my consciousness of my moments of existential pain, even though I have never seriously contemplated suicide. Although these processes of learning about life through living have been essential to the maturing of my work, I want to focus here on a larger process - that of how my personal journey into understanding and living my life more deeply has enriched and changed how I work with clients. Following are examples of several such larger processes which have transformed my life, and therefore my work.

One of the most significant of these processes is the impact of feminist ideas which began transforming my understanding of the politics of gender relations almost 20 years ago, and which have, in increasingly complex ways, expanded and informed my world view ever since. As I awakened to the ways in which gender oppression and dominant discourses about men and women shaped literally every aspect of my life in some significant way, I was, for the first time, able to begin liberating myself from these oppressive ideas. As I saw my own gendered experience with new eyes, so, too, was I able to see others, as well as the internalised gender beliefs which operate to maintain and support the external system of oppression. The more fully I understood the personal as political in my own life, the more fully I was able to recognise this phenomenon in the lives of others. The more actively I challenged gender oppression in its various guises in my own life, the more this awareness informed my therapeutic work. No longer could I work with an abused woman, for example, without being conscious of the forces of gender, economic, and social oppression which shaped her experiences, options, possibilities, choices, and her views of herself and her life. No longer could I see her and her relationships outside of the larger political context. As I learned to find my own voice in the midst of oppressive relationships, systems and organisations, I seemed increasingly able to help clients to find theirs, to claim their own lives, and to challenge the oppressive practices and systems which surrounded them.

My therapeutic work has also been shaped by my ongoing confrontation with my own life issues. As my ability to accept myself with empathy and non-judgement has grown, I have been able to listen to myself in new ways and to trust my own wisdom. As this trust in myself has grown, I have also developed absolute trust in the wisdom of my clients. As I have learned to allow myself to experience the full range of human emotion, including fear, sadness, anger, depression, grief, and despair, I have also been able to experience the fullness of joy and have developed an understanding and acceptance of pain as a natural part of life. This understanding has been essential to being able to be fully present with clients experiencing intense distress, and to trusting in their wisdom and in their ability to use life's challenges as opportunities for new learning and growth. It has also been essential to letting go of the illusion of expert knowledge, and to recognising each person's unique position as the true expert in their own life.

Finally, my work with clients has been deeply affected by my growing sense of spirituality over the past half decade. In some ways, this dimension is so all-encompassing that it could be seen to subsume everything else. It includes a fundamental respect for the divine within each of us and a view of each life as a spiritual journey, conscious or otherwise. For me it has involved finding new meaning in the processes of letting go, of practising non-attachment, of dealing with death, sickness and loss in life, of developing respectful, non-exploitative 'I-Thou' relationships (as described by Martin Buber 1984), and of enhancing and realising human potential. As my own life has become more inner-centred and calm, with a growing sense of purpose and meaning, I have found that I am more truly and fully present to clients and their lives. I hear differently and more deeply, with less inner chatter to distract me from hearing the nuances both of what is voiced and of what is unvoiced. I have begun to experience what I believe Buber meant by 'I-Thou' encounters in my conversations with clients. I have less need to know, to figure out, to be 'helpful' or clever, and more ability simply to be present, trusting in the client, the therapeutic process, and in myself, believing that the necessary words, connections and images will be there when I need them. Often I become aware of others' spiritual searching, of a hunger and seeking beyond what relationships, work or material success can offer. Increasingly, my conversations with clients may address questions of meaning and invitations to explore some spiritual practice such as meditation, journaling, or yoga. The reverence I feel for the strength and resilience of the human spirit fits well for me with narrative work, and with a belief in, and commitment to illuminating, stories of wisdom, courage, protest, and healing in people's lives.

How does my work affect me? Deeply and profoundly, often in ways beyond description. I am a different person because of it, and because of the people who share their lives with me. And, at the same time, my work grows and deepens and changes as I do. The complex interplay of these two processes is impossible to separate - each is part of the other, and together they make up a remarkably rich and privileged journey of ever-deepening exploration of what it is to be human.

Reference

Buber, M., 1984:
    I-Thou. UK: T. & T. Clark.

Acknowledgements

It is not possible to adequately acknowledge or name individually all those teachers, friends, colleagues, clients, students, and family members, who have inspired, influenced, supported, and nurtured my work and my journey over the past half-centruy. The following list is necessarily partial and incomplete.

First, I wish to acknowledge, with deep appreciation, all those who have shared their stories with me over the years, and inspired me with their courage and resilience. They have honoured me with their trust, and taught me about the ability of the human spirit to triumph and to flourish even in the face of overwhelming challenges.

I am also thankful for the many students who have questioned, pushed, explored, and examined, even my most dearly-held assumptions; who have taught me, by example, the power of curiosity; who have shared their ideas and their stories; and who have supported me, my work, and my ongoing evolution.

I am deeply indebted to my feminist teachers, colleagues, and friends: Helen Levine, Sandi Butler, Rachel Hare-Mustin, Dorothy Wheeler, Michele Bograd, Thelma Jean Goodrich, Lois Braverman, Daphne Hewson, Kerrie James, and Virginia Goldner, among others - who have taught me, by their example and their courage, to reject the path of comfortable acceptability, and embrace that of integrity and unpopular honesty - to name oppression, challenge the 'unchangeable', and claim my own voice.

I am also deeply grateful to my newest teachers, colleagues and friends: Michael White, Amanda Kamsler, David Epston, Kaye Stockell, Marilyn O'Neill, Charles Waldegrave, and Kiwi Tamasese, among others - who have taught me new ways of thinking and understanding, who have shared their work and ideas so generously with me, and who have warmly supported and encouraged my latest development and learning.

Finally, I must speak of the woman whose life has nurtured my own, and whose courage, resilience, and continued growth into old age, have inspired all who know her. My mother has been my lifelong teacher and friend. Long before the current feminist movement, she was introducing me to feminist ideas, and modelling the life of a woman who refused to bow to oppression. It was she who encouraged and supported my professional education, in spite of my father's disapproval of advanced education for women. It was she who understood my need to combine career and motherhood, long before it was accepted practice. Even now it is she who continues to teach me about the human potential for growth, pleasure, and vitality, across the whole of a lifetime regardless of disability and loss. And, finally, it is she who demonstrates so powerfully for me the ability to live fully in the present moment, and to accept with grace the changes and impermanence of life.

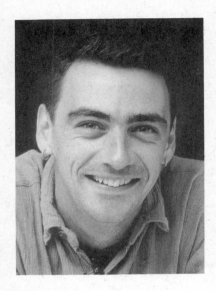

David Newman

By day, David is a social worker who has worked in the area of mental health and male sexual assault in Sydney for three years. *Editor's note: and by night he dreams of sailing the seven seas, in oceans as blue and as deep as his eyes.*

An Unspoken Connection

She will always carry on,
Something is lost, Something is found.
They will keep on speaking her name,
Some things change, Some stay the same.
(The Pretenders 1986)

It has, to a large extent, been an overly familiar and tedious story in my life - the story of self-doubt - and it is inevitably at play now as I sit down to write. It felt uncomfortably familiar when I was speaking with my friend David Denborough a few nights ago. As we spoke in our kitchen over a cup of tea, I found myself telling him of some of my successes in wrestling away from self-doubt by enlisting the support of my sister, Sally. 'Listen, I think this story would make a perfect addition to a collection of papers that I'm aware of', he said in his usual supportive enthusiasm. And of course I doubted him. Self-doubt loomed in my mind and took the form of likely outcomes if I was to start writing. 'You can't write', self-doubt informed me. 'You procrastinate too much to get around to writing. You don't really have anything particularly interesting or insightful to say.' And it kept on ... talking to me in such ways, mocking my efforts. However, it did not succeed in telling me everything about me, I guess, as I am now sitting and writing, something self-doubt would not have predicted.

I am conscious of providing self-doubt with too much space as I want to speak about some of the ways that I have beaten it and some of the ways I have embraced boldness. However, firstly I would like to outline the ways self-doubt interferes in my work as a social worker working with people with psychiatric diagnoses. It takes away my courage and energy.

Taking my Energy

If self-doubt creeps or even barges into my work, it takes away from my energy by saying things like, 'Given that you're not particularly good at what you do, why keep doing this work?' It distorts my understanding and has me looking at my work in ways that I am finding increasingly uncomfortable and unsuitable. These include ways that encourage me to compare myself with others, that encourage me to look at things that I have not been able to do instead of the things I have achieved, and that encourage me to be highly critical of my work. I can virtually always count on self-doubt to provide me with an analysis of a meeting with a client that goes something like, 'I think that meeting that you just did was about three-quarters as good as your last one, which means you may have slipped to the thirteenth best worker at this service. If you are able to study up a bit more you may get the skills to have perhaps an eight-out-of-ten performance at your next meeting with a client.' And so the dialogue goes on. Another common trick that self-doubt plays me is an unusual form of amnesia that means that I forget virtually all of my steps and accomplishments regardless of how thrilling they might have been for me. Or another trick again is trivialising my accomplishments by attributing them to others or external factors. This is not to say that I do not want to acknowledge the input of others in my life in things that I consider accomplishments. I find it less lonely and therefore generative to acknowledge the input of others in my life. I also think that it is largely through acknowledgement that we are able to understand our histories and how it is we are the people we are now. However, if I acknowledge others or external factors *at the expense* of my own input, then it can siphon my energy, making me less visible to myself.

Taking My Courage

If self-doubt creeps or barges into my work, it takes away from my courage by saying things like, 'You do not have the ability to express yourself coherently enough to invite this worker to consult with their clients about the effects of their ways of working'. Or another favourite is, 'I just can't find the exact words to make my point; I won't say anything as it won't come across perfectly'. The other effect of losing my courage is that it is somewhat destabilising of my perception of myself. If I see myself as a person with a commitment to standing up to and speaking against injustice, it is hypocritical to lose my courage when injustice is around me - injustice that includes belittling, trivialising or disrespectful ways of talking about the clients of our service. This hypocrisy gives self-doubt a stronger voice.

However, there is privilege for me in this notion of finding the exact words to say. The clients of our service do not have the same opportunity. The consequences for me of not finding courage, compared with the clients not finding their courage, are quite different. For me it may be a loss of face or a challenge to my worth as a 'professional' in my eyes or the eyes of other workers, yet for my clients the consequences can be more drastic. My clients' words are rarely heard as 'perfect'. Their sentences and experiences are regularly under scrutiny; they have less room to default on their courage and their battles can be a matter of life and death, as can be seen in the high number of suicides by people with psychiatric diagnoses.

From the Heart and Not Knowing

Self-doubt took such a shape for me as a young man largely in the confines of my school-yard. I recall being a student in a privileged all-boys high school at which we were being groomed to compete and to have a kind of self-assured air to our ways of being and talking, a certainty in ourselves and our knowledge. I remember schoolwork being like a small battle involving constant evaluation and the ranking of students. I also remember conversations or discussions being a process of 'point scoring', giving 'rational' opinions generally divorced from emotions, or a relentless 'putting down' of others and therefore deflecting attention away from oneself, away from one's insecurity. These were the means by which one became more sure of oneself, more certain, less vulnerable and therefore more respected as a young man.

Self-doubt revolved around an unhappiness with my rankings, but, also more commonly, not having the 'rational points' or 'truths' at hand in order to 'win an argument'. I remember that, often because I did not have the exact words in 'political discussions' with my peers, I would be silent. I understand now that there was a discomfort in my body at such intellectual, certain (or assured) ways of talking that seemed so emotionally disconnected from the issues being discussed. I have also come to understand that it is not rational ways of talking or being that are important to me. Now, standing up to self-doubt does not involve having the 'truth' at hand or being an expert. White men's expert knowledge has silenced too many for too long. Rather it involves an openness to 'not knowing', as Leela Anderson put it to me, and a boldness to speak from my heart.

A particularly powerful way that I have been able to undermine self-doubt and embrace boldness, or not knowing, has been with the support of certain friendships and lessons from my clients. I have also been able to utilise the support of my beloved sister.

An Unspoken Connection

I was born eighteen months after my sister, Sally. We shared a bedroom for the first eight years of my life. I recall that one of the most exciting opportunities this brought was to be able to occasionally turn on our bedroom light very early in the morning and play together with our dolls without waking our mother. Through the turmoil and battles of our childhood Sally was there alongside me, and I was there, I think to a less extent, alongside her. As a precocious child of eleven or twelve, she was the one to explain to me our mother's drinking problem. In the years that Sally and I lived alone with Mum, without our brother and sister, who were considerably older, she also helped me understand some of the baffling things that were happening in our home, telling me that it was all right and even understandable to be afraid of our mother.

Our mother died two days before my twelfth birthday, leaving us without parents. In the years following, whilst we were living with our grandmother and then with our older sister, we had long walks together, often beside the local river. Usually our poodle would be following, whining loudly, wanting someone to throw the ball for her and, although we would mostly tune out from her, we would occasionally oblige. We were able to talk openly in those times. I would hear from her about the dilemmas associated with attempting to have relationships with boys who were sexually and emotionally insensitive and at times abusive. And I would hear of the pain and difficulty she experienced around others' expectations of her academic performance at a private school, where she held a scholarship. (Her head-master made it clear to her what her problem was when he wrote on her Year 9 report that she was 'self-piteous'.) I also used to hear some of her experiences of experimenting with drugs. I must have been very concerned about the drugs, as I recall ringing up my brother when I first heard about her smoking 'pot', as our mother referred to it, and asking him to speak with Sally about her problem. In a conversation that required my brother to conveniently ignore his own drug-taking history, I do not think Sally was convinced of the perils of smoking marijuana.

As I got older, I would speak to Sally less openly, as I was starting to learn as a young man about the safety of isolation. Yet I would confide in her many of the difficulties I was experiencing. I would also speak of some of the positive things in my life, such as how I was doing well at school - but they somehow stand out less for me now. I have a card that Sally gave me for my fourteenth birthday that is still attached to my bedroom mirror. It captures some of our connection at the time:

Your future is dedicated to:

1) The love of Schnookems, [i.e. whining poodle who wanted ball thrown]

2) The love of your two sisters,

3) A new outlook, from your pessimism to a fully-qualified optimist, or could that be optometrist?

Without our relationship at the time, and messages such as this one, I wonder how much more momentum self-doubt might have gained?

Our isolation would have been profound if not for each other. I remember many times when Sally would enter my room. I would be in the middle of yet another engaging maths problem (later on I found morose music more engaging) and she would gently coax me out of my shell. It wasn't until many years later that I heard from one of Sally's closest friends at the time how she would tell her friends that she was proud of me and the way I was 'hanging in there' at school. She was proud of me when, with the exception of our brother and sister, there were very few others who would have had us in their hearts.

Sally used to introduce me to things I found threatening or difficult. Throughout our relationship she would invite me to confront my fears, and slowly I would push myself a little further. She bought me records by new bands such as The Specials, Nick Cave or The Pretenders, when I was used to listening to bands such as The Rolling Stones or The Beatles. Yet, in hindsight, the modern bands were far more interesting and, more importantly, provided credibility at school where knowledge of new music gave one 'cool' status. She would invite me into pubs, which terrified me when I was quite young, but had the same effect on my 'cool points tally' as knowing the latest groovy rock tune. What mostly comes to mind however was her 'project' for me. She knew that I was not experienced or particularly comfortable with physical contact or affection. One day I remember her clutching my hand, giving me a small kiss and telling me that she was going to help me warm to such contact.

A final story captures another aspect of our connection. One night when the two of us went out to dinner, at one point in the night we fell into silence. I remember never being comfortable with silence at the time, yet the silence between her and me did not concern me. I told her that I was not worried by our silence and she told me she had the same feelings. I guessed that we had a special connection, a connection that did not require words.

An Ending

When Sally died of a drug overdose at age twenty-three, as far as I was concerned we had lost that unspoken connection. All my hope for her retrieving her life from an overwhelming drug problem had gone. Although our relationship had been stretched and had had some difficulties, I was more isolated without her in this world. I still have difficulties understanding or thinking about how I'll never hear her musical laughter again, or witness her complete disregard for social etiquette that would make me laugh and fill me with pride in her courage to challenge conventions.

I have come to understand the impact on my life of Sally's going, and of losing our unspoken connection. One of the biggest difficulties for me is that I cannot be sure she is all right. In fact I picture her in a dark, cold and lonely place, still not experiencing the joys that I wish had been available to her whilst she was here. I also find it hard to accept that our relationship has ceased to exist, that it cannot continue from where it ended.

A Beginning

There are a few incidents that come to mind which have encouraged me to revisit our unspoken connection. The first was an opportunity to look at grief and loss differently in my life and in my work after reading an article on the subject by Michael White. I was particularly struck by the metaphor of 'saying hello' as opposed to the usual ideas and writings on the topic of loss and grief that encourage people to 'say goodbye'. The second was the encouragement of my friend at the time, Pia van de Zandt, to enlist Sally's support, especially in times of stress or when self-doubt reared its ugly head. Initially it was difficult, as I found myself thinking that our unspoken connection and her support were not accessible, and never would be again, since she was no longer with me in a physical sense. However, I came to see that our connection had changed but this did not necessarily deny me the ability to enlist Sally's support. With Pia's loving encouragement I began to feel warmth from the process of invoking Sally's support.

At the same time, encouragement came through my relationships with my clients. The ways in which we spoke of revisiting relationships that were not available to them for different reasons opened up space for me to do the same. One woman named Shannon particularly comes to mind. In 1992 Shannon moved to Sydney with her eleven-year-old daughter, having just separated from her husband. Shannon's relationship with her daughter was very important to her. Within a few months of moving, Shannon started hearing voices, and the local mental health service took her daughter from her. Her daughter had lived with her father ever since, and Shannon felt that their relationship had deteriorated greatly. When Shannon was referred to me two years later, one of the things we spoke about was the impact the voices had on her life. She told me that sometimes they were helpful for her, and she did not see their complete disappearance as a useful direction to move towards in our work together. Shannon informed me that one of the voices she heard was the voice of her daughter. When I asked her what that was like, she was in no doubt that it was a positive experience. She told me it brought her closer to her daughter and helped to keep the relationship alive. This experience played a large part in helping Shannon resume contact with her daughter, and they are now in regular contact, which she tells me has been enriching for both of their lives. Although the separation from her daughter was a painful experience for Shannon, the questions that honoured the positive effects of the voices and, in the process, invoked her relationship with her daughter, were invigorating for her. These questions helped bring their relationship together, and the process also somehow brought me closer to Sally.

Moving On

Presently, when self-doubt jumps on my back, I guess I have a way of asking myself a few questions or passing a few thoughts through my head. I ask myself things like: Would Sally think this is worth getting caught up in self-doubt? Would she think that self-doubt has absolutely nothing to offer me and that I could just laugh and shrug it off? I know she is pretty knowledgeable about my life and some of the things I might have going for me, so I wonder what good things she might see in me at the moment that have somehow become lost to me? When has she seen my boldness, recently and in the past? What would she say about the work that I'm doing? Would she be proud of me, perhaps, like she has been in the past? Or I ask myself questions such as: How can I work in ways that may assist people to avoid being engulfed in similar problems to the ones she had? And: What would it mean to me if I was able to make a positive difference to others' lives in a way that I did not seem to with Sally? The last questions brings with it sadness about how Sally's problems survived until her life ended, and occasionally with this sadness comes a self-accusation of inadequacy at not being able to assist Sally enough so that she could be here now to help me write this. The phrase 'what if' plagues me at times and, if it is combined with the voice of self-doubt, feelings of inadequacy can loom large. Yet the question also brings hope. To know that I may be assisting people in a way that helps them stand up to problems, some of them similar to the problems that Sally had, is an enormously invigorating experience that can drown out self-doubt and the accompanying feelings of inadequacy and lack of energy and courage.

As I have been writing this article, I have come to see there is another way that I challenge self-doubt and embrace boldness. This process involves consulting with my clients on their experiences of the mental health system. When they tell me the things they find helpful and unhelpful, I take their courage and knowledge with me into conversations with fellow workers, which encourages us to reflect on our work and to be more accountable to the people for whom we provide a service.

I am reminded of Michael's words. I had been working with him for some months around his problems with voices. We had spoken at some length about what he would like to see changed in the mental health system. He told me that the most important things he would like to see changed would be no file notes and more friendly communication from workers. When he became unwell and was admitted to hospital, I was able to speak with the admitting psychiatrist about some of Michael's knowledges and experiences of the negative effects of the mainstream mental health services, and how they could be more useful for him. Without having had the privilege of hearing these concerns and suggestions, I would not have been able to deliver as clear and direct a message. The psychiatrist told me he would not bring Michael's file into the interview; and he would have had a clearer understanding of the dilemmas for Michael in being admitted to an institution that has a long history of being experienced as uncaring and insensitive. To me this was a small but significant step. It was a step facilitated by Michael's generosity in trusting me with this information.

I find such conversations with workers invigorating, and when I take the voices and spirits of Sally and people like Shannon and Michael with me, I feel more courageous and less alone.

Seeing the effects of inviting clients to reconnect with, or 'say hello again' to, important relationships that are no longer available to them, has given me further inspiration to revisit my relationship with my sister. Their joys and battles will stay with me.

I cannot be sure Sally is in a place experiencing the joys that were mostly unavailable to her whilst she was here. I cannot be sure that she has friends where she is. However, when I revisit our connection, she brings me warmth, a certain magical strength; I feel my heart skip a beat and I can guess that she *is* OK. My relationship with Sally has continued. Our connection has survived her death and has been with me in some of my most difficult and enriching moments since then. We have moved on *together,* and my thoughts about her are not thoughts of loss or just past memories, but thoughts of how our connection is with me now, providing me with strength and inspiration to continue my work, helping me feel less isolated, and helping me finish this paper.

Reference

The Pretenders, 1986: 'Hymn to Her.' On compact disc, *Get Close.* Warner.

P.S.:

I guess it comes as a surprise to me, in many ways, that I am actually writing this finishing page. Apparently I was not going to be able to do this writing thing I told myself - I had no evidence from the past that I could. There is excitement for me in thinking about the words I have written and the different places it has taken me. And I ask myself, 'How did I get here? What happened along the way? and, What will it mean for me in my work?'

Writing the final draft of this paper, along with some conversations I have had, has helped me to notice the ripples that have found their way into my life, even in the short space of time since I wrote the initial draft. Friendships have been built or strengthened; old thoughts have been tossed aside with vigour and a certain sense of urgency; and it has brought connections, connections that are not loosened nearly as much as before by my habit of withdrawal. Also, as I re-read the first draft a month or two after I wrote it, I felt a lack of familiarity with the words - they did not speak to me as strongly as they had when I first wrote them. It seems that, in naming self-doubt, I had become somewhat distant from it, and it was also clear to me that I had moved on.

I have come to understand that, by writing this paper, I have been offered much by conversations with my clients, especially inspiration, knowledge, and encouragement, to re-visit connections. The ripples will affect my work with an increased awareness and acknowledgement of how I am touched in such ways by these conversations. And I can see that I will find my voice in the workplace.

When returning from holidays recently I was reminded of how I had moved on. I had a yearning to contact people, and my fingers did not hesitate over the buttons on my phone (yes, that has happened to me on more than one occasion). And the conversations have been lively and, in some cases, enriched by the knowledge of others having read my words - a richness that has taken me into the lives of others, and them into mine. Boldness has become a more familiar feature for me.

Acknowledgements

It is impossible to name all the people in my life who have invited me into boldness or who have helped me find connections, and it is impossible to capture all the ways that the following people have touched my life, but here goes. I want to thank:

Michael and Shannon for their generosity, courage and openness, and for inviting me into their joys and struggles, and enriching my life in ways that I am still coming to understand.

Other people with whom I have worked, whose stories are in my heart.

Sally Newman for our unspoken connection that has lived on.

Janine Doran for her generosity, consistency and love over the years. She has provided a solidity that has been a place for me to always return to, a solidity that has perhaps not been available to her.

James Doran for an emotional openness that has created space for me to do the same.

David Evans for the consistency and care of his friendship, and for having faith in me during some difficult times.

Pia van de Zandt for her care and loving encouragement to bring Sally back into my life.

David Denborough for his faith, love and encouragement. He has been present and wonderful in my moves towards boldness.

Sam Jennings for her passion, love and patience, and for helping me to see the shape of connection.

Cheryl White and Jane Hales for their friendship, generosity and gentle invitation to move on.

Mark Trudinger, Sam Wood and Mark D'Astoli for providing me with faith that connections can be built here.

Leela Anderson for her faxes, phone calls and comments on my paper, and finding the time to talk about these ideas over coffee.

Christian Beels

Chris Beels is a psychiatrist in private practice in New York City. He is on the faculty of the Ackerman Institute for Family Therapy, and spends as much time as he can painting.

Art, Government And Economy:
A book review

'The times are very evil'[1], and I find myself looking for an understanding of why, among other signs of meanness, there is an attack on psychotherapists, politicians, artists, and the institutions many of us work to improve. For some reason, I take this quite personally. One such reason is wanting to see my work, not as an individual effort to perfect an art, nor even as the project or property of a guild of therapists, but rather as a part of something larger, something in the interest of society as a whole. It was always very important to me, for example, that I worked most of my life in the Department of Mental Health of New York State. That department was as close as I could get, in this country, to working in the equivalent of the UK National Health or Australian government health services.

In the US, the press describes the vanguard of this attack on government responsibility as a group of romantic individualists whose idea of community is limited to the fundamentalist Christian Church (seat of so-called 'family values' such as opposing abortion), the embattled family members themselves, and the militias - the gun people who are trying to keep alive a vanished frontier. But more Americans than that voted to cripple the federal government in the last election. That Republican victory brings the probable-end of a whole range of institutions, from the National Endowment for the Arts to the Office of the Surgeon General, and the cutting back of environmental, workplace safety, and food safety programs, all in the name of the freedom of commerce.

Local governments also are carrying to extraordinary lengths the idea that commerce can provide social services. They are trying out 'privatisation' of prisons and police. And the Mayor of New York wants to sell the water supply to balance the budget. The most widespread and appalling change, however, and the one which has had the worst effect on the conduct of psychotherapy, is the move to turn the medical profession into a business run by insurance companies, and either bring psychotherapy under that yoke or isolate it as private practice. Insurance companies limit the choice of therapists a subscriber may consult to those on their panels, and may refuse, for example, to pay for 'talking' therapy if their regulations say that medication will be cheaper and equally effective. There seems to be general agreement that, under the 'squeeze' of insurance-company-managed care, very few therapists will be able to make a living from private practice.

I used to think of this movement as coming from a right-wing fringe group, but now our elected representatives are competing with each other to see who can take the most extreme of these positions. And the President, the leader of the opposition to the attack, is looking around to see what else he can give away to appease the armies at the gates, the crusaders whose banner is the sign of the dollar.

In this situation, I look around me and try to identify the 'us' who are being attacked. Who are we and what do we stand for? What is the city we defend, and why is it under siege? I also look at my own history of flight from the dominant culture that I grew up in, my wish to escape what seemed to me the heartless world of the Tulsa oil business for which my father and all our friends worked. I realise that I too am in danger of thinking in simplistic terms: I could withdraw into a religion of separation from the things that are Caesar's, a successor-religion perhaps to the Christianity which claimed to restrain the rapacity of the kings and nobles of Europe.

But then I realise that religion was very much 'in the world' of the medieval city. Are we the successors to the doctors, nuns, monks and friars, looking for the protection of the nobles and the merchants? In a godless and commercial time, who should care whether we preserve the libraries, sing the sacred music, run the hospitals, clothe the naked, feed the hungry, visit the sick, bury the dead, rebuke the tyrants, and go forth teaching the greater glory of God? Can that now all be done by the market?

I realise that, in order to think about all this differently, I need a natural history of what is, and is not, the market in the modern city. I need to understand what is the job of the market, and what is my job. I have found ideas about that in three books I have read over the last few years. None of them is remotely about family therapy, but they have helped to define the context of my professional work. All three were gifts from people important to me. I read them as bedtime stories that help me to lie down at night in the midst of the marketplace.

One reason I have been interested in these books is that they divide the market from the non-market world in ways that are new to me: neither worldly/spiritual, nor capitalist/communist, nor even patriarchal/feminist. There has always been something incomplete for me about those dichotomies, even though I have long felt that the feminist revolution was the best one going. But what, I have wondered, would still divide the world if that revolution succeeded? The world, capital, even some of men's preoccupations with hierarchy, territory, and power, are not 'wrong' - rather, they are out of place, elevated, idolised. They belong to the competitive world of the market, where they are merely the rules of the game. They become wrong when applied to other kinds of transactions. What kinds of transactions? Transactions between family members, perhaps are an example.

What these books have in common is a view of the market as a late and limited human invention, a specialised strategy for survival which today's crusaders have mistaken for the chief metaphor of all human endeavour: *homo economicus*. These authors describe a world where the market is alive and well, but confined, where capital flourishes, but not obscenely. Indeed, this other area that each book describes is a necessary and healthy complement to the market, perhaps even a holding condition for its survival.

The first is *The Gift: Imagination and the Erotic Life of Property* by Lewis Hyde. It was in fact a gift from a friend of mine who is a painter, who passed it along to me because it meant so much to him. I bought more copies and gave them to friends of mine. This passing along of gifts which the book inspires is also its subject: the history and rules of the gift economy. Hyde noticed a change in his view of his profession, writing, when he had not sold a book in a while and was beginning to worry about the experience of artists trying to survive in an economy of the market. He reflects on the fundamental contradiction of the idea of art as a market commodity.

Art, he says, is a gift - it is part of the gift economy. In most societies art is not sold, but given by the artists. The artist is not a specialised professional person, but someone recognised as having, her/himself, a 'gift' to give - a talent for ornament or dance or song. In these societies, art and religion go hand-in-hand as gifts, devotions, as indeed they did in our own society in eras when the artist worked for a patron who saw the purpose of his (usually his) sponsorship of the art as a gift, if not to God and the Church, then to the greater glory of some other larger entity, the City or the Family. This is parallel to the West Coast Native American institution of the Potlatch, the massive giving of treasure to other tribes, in which the Big Man is known by the magnitude of what he gives away.

Hyde's book, along with the other two I will describe shortly, is partly concerned with money and lending. Hyde notes that the medieval prohibition of usury was a prohibition which only extended to the edges of the tribe or family. You could not charge interest to a member of your own family because the loan to your own relative had to be a gift, not a way of making money. Extending the concept of family to the edges of the tribe, Jews could charge interest to Christians, but not to each other. The great achievement of the Calvinist divines of the early eighteenth century was to declare interest lawful between any lender or borrower, sanctifying the basis of the modern banking industry. Ezra Pound, one of the many writers and poets discussed in this book, took that subject up again, railing against usury as the root of evil.

In his exploration of the history of art versus commerce, Hyde describes the operation of the gift economy in many societies. He illustrates its assumption that what is given will be given away again, and, in this spiritual sense, will return to the giver with increase. It is the exchange basis not only of art but of education and learning as well. Its model is the giving relation between family members and the family as a whole. These transactions are different from those of the market, where increase comes from profit at the margin, or of banking where it comes from expanding debt. In both cases the relationship is a contract rather than, as in the gift economy, a devotion of the heart. When the two economies are confused and the rules of commerce are applied to the giving of gifts, art and learning suffer a degradation and decline.

The second book, Jane Jacobs' *Systems of Survival*, calls the area that is not commerce 'guardianship'. Her sub-title is *A Dialogue on the Moral Foundations of Commerce and Government,* emphasising that politicians' first responsibility is to be guardians, and that one of the things they need to guard is the distinction between the market and non-market parts of society. She writes in the delightful form of a fictional dialogue between a group of articulate modern women and men who have a series of weekend meetings at which they discuss the rules, the ethical assumptions, and the special concerns and purposes which characterise commerce on the one hand and guardianship on the other. For example, they talk about the difference between telling lies in two types of transactions, banking and diplomacy. Deception is clearly something that both the bank officers and the account-holders regard as punishable. You go to jail for embezzling or forgery, and you are fined for an overdraft. Deception is against the basic assumptions of a business contract. There are times, however, when deception is essential to the conduct of diplomacy, and both sides know it, since governments see themselves as having major commitments to the guardianship of their peoples that override the rules of honesty.

Some institutions of guardianship, such as Congress or the police, cannot do their work as businesses. Police officers doing business are corrupt by definition. Even giving the police a business-like ethos, for example by setting productivity goals, leads immediately to injustices such as false arrest. On the other hand, the history of communism shows the failure of guardianship to arrange a better, or even fairer, distribution of goods than the market.

The wonderful thing about this book is that it faces the enormous complexity of the relations and differences between the two kinds of enterprise, painting neither as good or bad, but emphasising the consequences of muddled thinking and confusion between the two. Like Hyde, Jacobs sees the destructive consequences of mixing the moralities of the two areas. The Mafia, for example, is a guardian organisation which traffics in commerce. And the cutting down of the safety net since the last US election is an example of what happens when the government's guardian responsibility is given over to the bankers. Jacobs is ingenious at revealing the way social institutions work -

here and in her previous books about the vitality of cities. Margaret, my wife, has been feeding me Jacobs' books for many years and they are wonderfully sustaining.

And finally I want to tell you about *For the Common Good* by Herman E. Daly and John B. Cobb. Jr. It is subtitled *Redirecting the Economy toward Community, the Environment, and a Sustainable Future.* It was given to me by my son-in-law, an environmental policy professional, and a member of a generation that will have to try to rescue the promise of that subtitle from the recklessness with which my generation has wasted it. Daly was his professor at the University of Maryland, and was previously a senior economist at the World Bank. Cobb is a theologian.

The authors are proud to be capitalists, since clearly the market that we now have works arguably better than any other method of distribution. But the point of this book is that a religious belief in the market - an ignorance of the extent to which the market needs to be protected against its own limitations and natural failings - is a threat to the common good of which the market is a part. Markets, as Adam Smith understood, create the conditions for their own demise if they are allowed to run without limits, and we now are aware of some limits which Smith did not know: the limits to growth brought about by internationalisation of capital, and the escape of corporations from an obligation to benefit the country, the community, in which they operate. This is the point made by Aristotle, the first economist: *oikonomia* is properly the study of the laws of all the environmental factors that influence the health of the nation-household, over the long term. It has little to do with the short-term dynamics of personal wealth, which our modern economics departments and advisers have elevated to an idolatrous worship of a golden calf.

This is a very scholarly book, an education in economics all in itself, and a rich pleasure to read. It could be the basis of a political party platform, a reasoned proposal about what can be done now before things get irreversibly worse. The last chapter, 'Money, debt and wealth', makes an essential point, that money is only an invention, like fire and the wheel. And great as the benefit is that has come from it, more people have been destroyed by the fluctuations of money than have been crushed by the wheel or burned by fire. The religious belief in the infinite expendability of debt, which is at the heart of our plan for our future, is criticised with a mathematical clarity that even I could understand. Usury may not be the root of all evil, but it certainly needs watching.

The authors see themselves and others writing in this area as part of a modern prophetic tradition, urging the people to turn from idolatry. The next to last chapter, 'The religious vision', holds out the possibility that: *on a hotter planet, with lost deltas and shrunken coastlines, under a more dangerous sun ... a legacy of poisonous wastes, and much beauty irretrievably lost ... our children's children will learn at last to live as a community among communities.*

I understand, as Michael Lerner says, that the reason the people of our country voted in such large numbers for the golden calf is that our political prophets have failed them, have failed to give them the vision without which the people perish. They have come to believe that their only hope is in making money and keeping the heathen off their land. Is there any way they could hear this book's message?

These books help me to persevere in doing therapy with families because they tell me what forces are operating in concert with what I am trying to do. They also tell me where the market-workers in these families get their images from. I have even given copies of *The Gift* to a few hard-working fathers, and they have found it arresting. For some, it has helped them to understand the possibilities of giving in their relationships with people close to them, with whom they cannot afford to have a market exchange.

References

Daly, Herman E. & Cobb, John B. Jr. 1994:
  For the Common Good: Redirecting the economy toward community, the environment, and a sustainable future. Boston: Beacon Press.
Hyde, Lewis, 1983:
  The Gift: Imagination and the erotic life of property New York: Vintage (Random House).
Jacobs, Jane, 1992:
  Systems of Survival: A dialogue on the moral foundations of commerce and government. New York: Random House.
Lerner, Michael, 1995:
  Address to the Family Therapy Networker Conference, Washington DC, March 23.

Nguyen Phan thi Ngoc Dung

Dung is a Vietnamese refugee who grew up in South Vietnam during the Vietnam war then went to France and Australia. She has studied psychology and education and worked as a teacher of languages, an interpreter and a counsellor. Dung is committed to the respect of human rights in Vietnam and the welfare of Vietnamese refugees, and is interested in cultural issues, global exchange, and sharing of cultural ideas and spirituality (especially Buddhism and Zen Buddhism).

Reconnections And Changes

One of the gestures I remember vividly from my childhood is the image of my mother bowing to greet her friends and relatives. She would have her hands joined as in prayer, she would humbly and respectfully bow down, head and shoulders lowered, while her face lit up in a most gracious and welcoming smile. Middle-aged and old men and women in my country do the same when they greet people in the traditional way. As a child, I too was taught to cross my arms and bow down to greet my parents' friends and relatives.

Once I accompanied my mother to a Buddhist temple. She respectfully bowed down to the Buddhist monk. He would reciprocate while saying the name of the Buddha: A Di Da Phat (Amitabha). My spiritual teacher later explained to me that Buddhists believe that everyone, even the most sinful person, has deep in their heart the Buddha Nature. Everyone is Buddha in essence and in becoming. Thus, when the Buddhist monk bows to everyone he meets, he is saying, 'You are Buddha and I respectfully greet you'.

When I grew up, western thoughts and ideas started to influence our culture and way of life. I was unable to join my hands in prayer and bow down to greet my friends and relatives the way my mother did. I found it hard to kow-tow or to prostrate myself before the Buddha or the ancestors' altar. My western education saw it as a symbol of demeaning oneself and of self-abdication.

Now that I practice narrative therapy, the importance of the sense of respect I owe my clients reconnects me to my cultural heritage. I can sincerely join my hands in prayer and bow down to people to greet them. I establish right from the beginning a respectful relationship. I consider their feelings and personal opinions and use words that will not hurt them.

I now understand that the way I look at people influences their self-image, their self-esteem, and their confidence. Societal and familial cultures, ideologies and beliefs construct our selves, but at a micro-level other people's gaze also moulds us. If that gaze is respectful, we will respect ourselves, we will feel confident and powerful. If that gaze is arrogant or demeaning, we will retract in self-doubt, in self-deprecation and powerlessness.

I once thought that respect was only due to the elders, the knowledgeable and wise persons, the 'authorities'. I now think that respect is due to everyone, just because s/he is a person, whether a child, an old person, 'mentally ill', healthy, rich or poor. In each individual lies a source of resourcefulness and wisdom worthy of respect. What made this shift possible? I think the link between respect and work was highlighted when I watched Michael White working with a couple who had schizophrenia. I then realised that the respect Michael showed to this couple contributed significantly to their growing confidence and self-esteem. That respect enabled them to get in touch with their own strength and healing powers. I remember that I once spoke to two street youths in Vietnam. They were having a brawl and I tried to appease them. I spoke to them in a calm, sweet and polite tone. The next day, one of them came to my house and said, 'I was never respected by anyone except you. No one has ever spoken to me the way you spoke to me. Thank you.' I understood that he yearned for the respect long due to him. Now, when I work with my clients, I believe in them and I respect them. The response is therapeutic, boosting confidence, self-esteem, self-worth, self-respect and even joy.

Working and using the ideas of narrative therapy has enabled me to re-connect with my own lost sense of self-respect. My culture taught me to discount women and myself. Confucianist teaching said that when a girl is a child, she follows her father, when she gets married, she follows her husband, when her husband dies, she follows her eldest son. In the couple's relationship, the husband is in the driver's seat and the wife is a 'lesser-being'. Yet a popular Vietnamese saying reveals an 'alternative story': it says, 'If there is agreement and harmony between the husband and the wife, they can even empty the South China Sea'.

Now that I listen to women who tell of their sufferings in a patriarchal relationship, I can see myself through their eyes. I can see where my mother was and where I am. It is as if, for the first time, I step out of myself and look back at me, at my life, not through the lenses of the dominant ideology, but through the lenses of feminism and its interpretation of power. When the light of truth strikes, it dissipates fear. A sense of peaceful strength and courage wells up in me. I am now starting to deconstruct the dominant ideology that is enslaving and deprecating women. I want to reclaim my self-respect, my preferred identity, my happiness and my life. It means I will consider my own needs as well as other people's needs. The importance of harmony and co-operation in my culture makes me fight non-violently and patiently.

Buddhism has always taught me self-awareness. In meditation, when I breathe out, I know that I am breathing out. When I breathe in, I know that I am breathing in. In everyday life, when I am angry, I know that I am feeling angry or I know that I am having depressing thoughts, etc. A Buddhist saying is that 'One only needs to turn one's head to see the shore of liberation'.

Narrative therapy again reconnects me to another aspect of my cultural heritage.

Self-awareness is a meta-cognition mood where I can put a distance between myself and a problem and thus look at it from afar. Self-awareness helps me to deconstruct the problem. Distancing from my problem also means self-control and freedom.

To turn one's head, in the Buddhist saying, now means to me to have another look at life, to look at the alternative story - one that is in harmony with self-care, happiness, self-respect, compassion and harmony.

The narrative way of working has enabled me to learn and experience the value of unconditional, non-judgmental love. I once naively categorised people as good and bad. Good people deserved love and respect. Bad people deserved ill-feelings and disrespect. I now think that people are good in some ways and towards some people. At the same time, they are bad in other ways and towards some other people. Life is multi-storied and character is also multi-storied. I now believe that everyone needs and deserves unconditional love and respect. Unless I give such love and respect, I cannot foster and encourage the growth of the alternative story in people I work with.

Helen O'Grady

Helen O'Grady has an academic background in politics. She currently lives in Adelaide, working as a counsellor in the area of women's health. She has recently received a scholarship to do a PhD, the focus of which will be Foucault, narrative therapy, and feminist theory.

A Beginner's Story

I am a newcomer to the area of counselling. The narrative therapeutic approach is the only type of training I have. Nonetheless, even at this early stage, I am aware of some of the profound and transformative effects this work has had on my beliefs and thinking, and my life generally. Some of these effects became apparent very early on in my training as we began to see people who consulted us about their lives, and others have only gradually become visible to me over time. Perhaps I will start with an account of the former and end by recounting those more gradual effects.

When I decided to change work directions from academia to counselling, a number of people commented that the main problem I would probably face was the potential to get burnt out, listening to other people's (often complex and seemingly insurmountable) problems all day long, perhaps not being able to really make much of a difference a lot of the time. These people weren't counsellors themselves but had known or heard about counsellors, social workers and/or other health workers who had faced such problems. Perhaps forewarned is forearmed, and I kept these comments in mind.

There was one thing, however, that no-one warned me about, and that was the high probability of being deeply moved in this kind of work. As we began seeing people in our training, and when I began one-to-one counselling with women, I experienced time and time again a deep sense of being moved by the stories of people's lives, and the courage and strength they revealed in making stands against the effects of various kinds of abuse on their sense of self, their relationships and their lives generally. I began to realise that although, in a very real sense, the human spirit is fragile and can be deeply wounded by careless and abusive behaviour, it can also be indomitable. The people I see consistently bear witness to this.

One example that comes immediately to mind is a young woman who recounted a story about how, at the age of five, in the face of extreme physical and emotional abuse at home, she sought out what she called 'positive attention' by becoming involved in running at school. She had noticed that children who did well at running got this kind of attention. In her very first race she ran and ran, and then became aware there was no-one else around, and thought she must have run off the track. Confused, she sat down by the side of the road and after a while she noticed the other children running up the track. Suddenly it dawned on her she had actually been winning the race, and she jumped back up and kept on running. She came first. She explained to me it was because she was desperate to get some positive attention that she had been able to run so fast and hard - she simply had to win. After this, with encouragement from a teacher, she achieved on-going success as a runner. Although these achievements were ignored by her family, they helped to counterbalance the effects of the abuse on her sense of self.

This story has touched me deeply. Each time I recall it I see in my mind's eye a small child literally 'running for her life', determined to keep her young spirit alive in the face of constant abuse at home where she had no power to change what was happening to her. Each time I recapture this image I am filled with a sense of awe at this child's refusal to be completely quashed by the abuse, and I am connected with a stronger sense of hope for the spirit of other children in similar situations. This knowledge of her helps me to understand the types of resources this now young woman is able to draw on in her current struggle to get her life back from the impact of abuse.

This is just one of many powerful stories I have been privileged to hear. And as I came to realise that feeling deeply moved is a constant factor in this work, I began to wonder how many people could name this as a feature of their work. Perhaps some people would feel relieved at the absence of opportunities for such strong feeling in their work. After all, it might be a risky proposition to have one's emotions brought so powerfully to the fore. I think there is a risk. It has to do with experiencing a feeling of interconnectedness with others in relation to our common humanity; it involves us leaking out of our own edges, moving beyond ourselves and connecting with others on a level of shared feeling. Despite the risks, however, I have experienced a sense of relief and appreciation as this capacity has been awakened in me. It has made me realise that I am capable of deeply felt emotions in my interactions with others, and because of this I am able to experience and use much more of myself in this work. This means I'm not restricted to just using my intellectual faculties but have the opportunity to work on a number of different levels. The risk associated with this, it seems to me, is that the 'comfortable' feeling of separateness from others, which is encouraged in our individualistic culture with its expert-oriented professionalism, can no longer be so easily maintained. For me, therefore, it's about daring to feel, and coming to understand that, just by virtue of being human, there are common bonds of empathy which allow us to be touched by and to touch each other's lives in ways that can make a difference to us all.

A second and related aspect of this work has been the gift of inspiration. Whenever I saw people, either in my training or in my own work, I initially got this funny sense that someone had gone out and hand-picked the most amazing people and asked them to come in in order to give me, the 'new' counsellor, an inspirational boost. Of course this wasn't true! But it made me realise that working with people in respectful and acknowledging ways, which don't assume we have the answers to their problems, invites recognition of what is remarkable about people and, in this way, opens up the possibility for inspiration on a routine basis.

In much the same way as we often feel inspired by certain books and films which give us a fresh surge of energy and enthusiasm for our life, the people I see provide a constant source of inspiration. Bearing witness to people's struggles and the changes they make in the process of reclaiming their lives for themselves and those they love, frequently against great odds, acts as a powerful encouragement about what is possible in this work. In this way I gain an accumulation of knowledges from the people with whom I work. This broadens my understanding of what is involved in their particular struggle, as well as revealing that there are often common threads over a range of presenting issues. I am then in a position to pass on something of their experience to others on similar journeys. This is not to say that every person's experience will be the same, but that people often find it acknowledging and encouraging to know that others have experienced similar problems and have been able to move beyond these obstacles and towards their own goals; sometimes strategies used by one person can also fit for others.

Another facet of witnessing people's struggles and triumphs in this work is that I am able to build up substantial reserves of hope about what is possible for people's lives. To see a woman who has taken her life back from the near-starvation effects of an eating disorder, or to witness a survivor of child abuse move towards self-belief and self-love, cannot but fuel hope. I believe this sense of hope has become part of my general orientation towards the work; its presence, often unspoken yet tangible, gets imparted to those with whom I work, and in this way contributes to a sense of optimism about the possibilities for different lives.

Because of the importance of people's contributions to my work in these ways, I feel it is important to acknowledge this by sharing with them what it has been like for me to hear their story and witness their struggles and steps towards what they want for their lives, and how what I have learnt from them contributes to the effectiveness of my work. Often people are completely unaware of *their* contribution to the therapeutic interaction, and are quite taken aback to learn of it. My original motive for sharing this information lay in a wish to acknowledge their contribution to my work, in a similar way to academic referencing of other people's ideas in written work. But I have come to realise that such acknowledgement can also have unexpected effects. When I imparted to one woman my experience of working with her over a number of months and asked her how she would feel about being part of my (mental) team when I was working with other women in her situation, her response caught *me* unawares. Her eyes filled with tears and she said I couldn't know what my request meant to her. She explained to me that she had always been put down for being unworldly; she was perceived as being capable of being at home and looking after children, but she had never felt she had a place 'in the world'. She said my request gave her the opportunity to stand 'in the world'. As she spoke, I became aware of how profound this was for her, and I felt privileged to witness the intensity of her emotion. I joked lightly about how bad the pay was for physically invisible team members, but she told me there was no price I could pay her that would be worth more than what I had offered. She also said that she did want to help other women but that she did not currently have the energy to do this directly. Being in the room with me in spirit as I worked with others, however, she said, was an ideal way for her to do this indirectly. Her response reinforced for me the importance of never assuming that people are aware of their contribution to the therapeutic relationship, and how beneficial this information may be to the development of alternative stories of people's lives.

To talk only about people's contribution to my work, however, would be to leave a story half untold. For my interactions with people who consult me about their lives also inspires me to think about my own life, and how I can make changes that bring me closer to what I want for myself and those I love. So many times a phrase uttered, or a description someone uses to convey their experience or beliefs, captures something really important about my own experience and is deeply acknowledging of it. This allows me later to shine new light on old ways of looking at things; and it can open up a myriad of possibilities for change that simply weren't available to me before. When one woman said she had always known that she would never be able to have marriage and a family of her own because of what had happened in the past, I, too, realised there were a number of things I had always assumed were beyond my reach because I felt undeserving of them - for example, having children. These assumptions had lain half-hidden, and therefore obscured, before this woman's words brought them out into the light. Once this idea was uncovered, I was able to ponder how it could be that I have harboured such beliefs. How might I go about changing them so as to free myself from such limitations on my life, and move closer to having genuine choices?

Similarly, sometimes while walking to the train station after a session with someone, I realise that I, too, have been up against a lot in my life in trying to get free from the effects of some intensive training in self-negation, both as a female in patriarchal culture, and from my early religious upbringing. Gaining this clarity helps to free me from the idea that self-negating stories speak the truth about myself. It allows me to acknowledge the many times I have stood against such stories and moved towards self-acceptance and self-belief. It generates a fresh surge of energy for ongoing acts of resistance to further diminish the hold self-negation has on me. These are some of the things I get from this work.

When I talk with women about the effects of our sessions on me, I share my experience of having felt inspired both for my own work and in my own life. The response is often one of surprise, because the prominence of cultural ideas of professionals as experts often has people assuming that counsellors know all the answers to people's problems and, moreover, don't have any issues of their own. Nonetheless people usually seem pleased to know of their contribution and appreciate having this acknowledged. And for me, acknowledging what I get out of the work, on both a professional and a personal level, goes some way to redressing the power imbalance inherent in the therapeutic relationship.

The effects of training and working as a narrative counsellor that I have so far described have been evident from quite early on. Other effects have been more gradual. The gradual nature of their impact, however, doesn't really surprise me, as they involve a questioning of deeply ingrained cultural practices. First, the notion that we are individuals is such a taken-for-granted part of our identity in contemporary white western societies that it is difficult to take a step back and hold this notion up for critical examination. Yet, when I do attempt this, I can see that there are certain dominant culturally constructed meanings associated with our idea of individualism which have more to do with conformity than personal uniqueness. An example of this relates to cultural prescriptions of self-possession or self-containment (White 1994, p.73). This particular prescription has captured my attention because I have become aware that the price of self-possession is the silencing of other possible ways of being an individual which may, in fact, be more fulfilling. It seems to me that being self-possessed fits most easily with western male, middle-class, liberal notions of detached reason. This is the group which has had the power historically to have its particular views generalised as the 'truth' or the 'natural' account of things (Foucault 1986, pp.54-5, 73-4). Possession or containment of ourselves is supposed to represent a mark of our ability to honour our rational capacity for thinking through our own beliefs and plans for our life rather than accepting uncritically the views of others. In this way we can be seen as self-determining. But in this view rationality tends to get defined in a narrow way, divorced from passion and emotions which are seen to cloud our ability to make (detached) reasoned judgements. Thus it is a type of reason that attempts to step back from who we are as whole persons, and as such has us separated from various aspects of ourselves. In addition it seems to me that this particular way of marking ourselves out as autonomous from others and/or prescribed views involves taking on board an exaggerated sense of separation between ourselves and others which denies the possibility of a fundamental connectedness between us.

If a therapist accepts the achievement of self-possession as the hallmark of good mental health, what is this belief endorsing and therefore imposing on the people who consult us? What risks does this view run of reproducing the very ideas and beliefs which may have caused problems for someone in the first place? Immediately I think of people from non-Anglo backgrounds, although it can also relate to a number of people and groups within mainstream Anglo culture. One startling example of this is given by Michael White in his account of working with a man who had become skilled in acts of self-torture during a long career in the psychiatric system:

> In his attempts to achieve a sense of moral worth in his community, he had been operating on his thoughts, his body, his lifestyle, his soul and so on. He had been doing all of this in the name of self-possession, self-containment, self-dependence and so on - nothing special you know,. just the sort of specifications for personhood that are valorised in our culture. (White 1994, p.81)

For myself, being enculturated into the idea that a 'proper' person is self-contained or self-possessed has often had me feeling that I can't quite 'make the grade' when I have judged myself, or been judged by others. Such is the power of ideas and practises when they take on the status of 'truth claims' rather than just one possible way of being which may or may not fit for people. They can have us turning ourselves inside out, taking on a career as a contortionist as we twist and turn and bend ourselves to try and fit into something that is basically ill-fitting in terms of the way we experience ourselves as persons.

Getting clearer about how the idea of separateness was ill-fitting for me has played an important part in initiating a reconnection with my daughter, whom I gave up for adoption 24 years ago. This step of reconnection was something I had vowed I would never do. I had always held a clearcut view about this situation which was shaped by a notion of the rights of autonomous individuals. I felt I had given up any rights of contact with my daughter by making the decision to give her up for adoption. She had had no say in this decision which would affect her life in fundamental ways. Up until recently, I believed that initiating contact with her as an adult would be an infringement of her rights. This made a lot of sense to me intellectually and fitted with my sense of justice and respect for her privacy. Looking back, I can see how this perspective made the situation very black and white, leaving no room for shades of grey.

As I began to think about and embrace the idea of connectedness rather than simply individual rights and autonomy, my view of what was possible changed. I began to acknowledge the importance of my connection with my daughter, which was so abruptly cut off at birth and emotionally shelved for many years, and her connection to me as her birth mother. And I was able, albeit tentatively and with some ambivalence, to initiate contact. This is a very recent event and I am not yet able to know fully what it means for either of us. But it has been a life-changing event for me. First and foremost it has been incredible to know that my daughter did in fact grow up in a loving family environment, loved and accepted for who she is, and that she has had a range of choices about her life. This is the hope that sustains you when you give up a child, but you never know if it's just a fantasy you have to believe to justify your decision. Secondly, there is now the possibility of developing a relationship with my daughter, a prospect which fills me with hope and joy.

All this is not to say that I think rights are unimportant. Rather, the way we generally understand them in our individualistic culture is within a prescribed framework that privileges abstract formalised principles and the idea of autonomy in terms of separation between persons. And what this can tend to do is preclude an emphasis on connectedness and particularity (Gilligan 1982). For me, moving from a focus on rights to thinking about the connection between my daughter and me has opened up possibilities that I hardly dared dream of before.

In some ways this too is another new beginning for me, like counselling. In other ways it is a story that began a long time ago. Since her birth, my daughter has always been part of my life. Our new beginning now is built upon a re-emerging history of conscious connection, a connection once blurred by separation. It is a beginning within already-established beginnings, yet its particular shapes and contours will be its own, as our physical presence in each other's life redresses the past and builds a bridge towards an unknown future of possibilities.

References

Foucault, M. 1986:
: 'Truth and power.' In Rabinow, P., *The Foucault Reader*. Penguin.
Gilligan. C. 1982:
: *In a Different Voice: Psychological theory and women's development*. Cambridge, MA: Harvard University Press.
White, M. 1994:
: 'Interview with Michael White and the narrative perspective in therapy.' Interviewed by Bubenzer, D., West, J. & Boughner, S. *The Family Journal*; 2(1):71-83).

Acknowledgements

I would like to thank Ellen and Thomas for teaching me about love and connection, and helping me on my way in the world. Though they themselves have long departed, their spirit continues to live on, enriching and sustaining my life.

Three generations on, I would like to thank Kerri - for being the person she is and, in particular, for her generosity of spirit in accepting me into her life.

Vonnie Coopman-Dewis

I first entered university (1973) as a student of archaeology. Later I chose to work with live bodies, not dead ones, and became a physiotherapist. But I missed the searching for fascinating stories, through archaeology. So I became a counsellor and through narrative study I joyfully find myself again an 'archaeologist'.

After the transplant from me to him

My brother died
7.10 am yesterday;
Sunday....
So I went to
work today
perhaps because
my most loved
customer
was due in at 10.00 am.

She didn't show
and
I couldn't help feeling
my brother
saved her

and left me
to the counsel
of an empty chair

He always was
wise.

After years of professional isolation

I didn't
just come here
to learn.
I came to
become
part of the
spirit
of things
and
in this
I believe
I have learned
more
than clever
professional practice.

Can You Guess the Dominant Colour of My Culture?

I wanted to look
good
for my interview
today.
So I tried to buy
a pair of flesh coloured
stockings
to wear with my
new frock.
I couldn't find any
so
I wore
black stockings
instead.

Consulting me about her sadness

'And when was the last time
you really experienced
some gaiety
in your life
Susan?'

'I mean
you've spoken of a partner -
What might
he
be able to tell me
about you -
when gaiety has been
more a part
of your life?'

'Well,
Wendy
has been with me
for 7 years
and I think she'd say
I find it hard
being
Gay!'

Self-actualisation

If you want
to self-actualise
just read
The DSM-IV.
You're sure to
'find yourself'
somewhere!

Susi Chamberlain

Susi Chamberlain is a family therapist and counsellor located in Canberra, where she has a private practice and teaches at the University of Canberra on the post-graduate counselling course.

The Barber Sang On Sunday

Yesterday I heard a refrain which cast me back into the Sundays of my childhood. Someone was playing an aria from *Il Barbiere di Siviglia* and I instantly sniffed again the scents of freshly washed children, starched clothes, Apple Blossom perfume, and a trace of Californian Poppy. Every Sunday morning, as I helped my young brothers and sisters get ready for Mass (hair brushed, faces washed, clean clothes on), Dad would have The Barber on the record player. Tito Gobbi or Luigi Infantino would sing the 'Largo al Factotum', or whisper about whispering as a means of political control in 'La Calumnia'.

Mass was in Latin in the fifties and sixties, but we went to a special service at Sacred Heart in which the sermon and the readings were in Italian. The congregation rustled with whispered comments, the women were almost all dressed in black, both sexes of adults seemed to have moustaches, and we sang 'Faith of our Fathers' in Italian.

At Easter or on the Sundays close to family birthdays, all the family would gather at our house for a late lunch. I was the second eldest of forty-five first cousins, and these gatherings would mean that I would have salads to make or chickens to roast or potatoes to peel, little children to mind, nappies to change, or dishes for sixty people to wash up after the meal. But somehow there was always time for some play and laughter, and singing was mandatory.

Easter was a particularly busy time for the extended family. We would gather from the oldest to the youngest to make the salami, prosciutto, pancetta and other pork products which would last us until the following year. Some of the men would be making the new wine, and some of the women the cheeses, ricotta and the forms of fresh new cheese which would yellow and harden over the year. The kids would race around with the salt, pepper, spices, garlic, or the long intestine casings, getting underfoot or being helpful by turns. And when everything was cleared up, we'd all grab a plate of pasta and the adults would have a few glasses of wine and someone would call out 'Give us a song, Bert!', and my Dad would raise his voice in 'Funiculi, funicula!' or 'Tiritomba' or 'Nessum Dorma', and everyone would sing until midnight. But this was only where and when it was safe - amongst family - to be Italian.

I was born in Melbourne in 1950; Dad is Italian, Mum is sixth-generation Irish-

Australian. Neither set of grandparents approved of their child's choice of partner, so from the very beginning I lived in the liminal space between two cultures. When I went to school, I discovered that the Italianness I had accepted as normal was considered to be strange, abnormal and inferior. I can still see the face of Mother Marie-Therese who caught me putting my salami-in-vienna-bread sandwich into the bin uneaten. She raged at the waste of food. I stoically took the disgrace because it was the lesser shame in comparison with the ridicule of my peers for eating 'wog food'. I was six.

Within a few years of being at a good Anglo-Celtic Catholic school, I had learnt the lessons of shame extremely well. Catholic guilt and cringing about being a Dago were compounded by the sneers of my class-mates - it was a reality not just a feeling! - into a personal worthlessness, which I interpreted by age ten to be my fate. Adolescence brought rebellion, a disdain for everything Italian, and a fierce juvenile feminism, all secretly mixed with a yearning to be acceptable. The tools I had were my intellect and my determination. I took on two enemies at once - the patriarchy through an unyielding commitment to get to University and the Establishment by acquiring a Trinity College accent through speech lessons. I became the most obnoxious superior pompous prig in my late teens - I could almost have qualified for a place in the dominant culture. With absolute contempt for my heritage, everything Italian became inferior in my own eyes. Only what the English establishment had to offer could be considered worthy of achievement. The family's fortunes were variable in those years - millionaires one decade and in poverty the next - so class was negotiable as long as I hid the unfortunate nature of my bicultural background.

Fortunately, I failed to get my arts degree in the late 1960s and was forced to go to work to support myself. While the majority of jobs I took on were clerical, I also experienced life on the factory floor, in retail, door-to-door selling, cleaning, etc. My favourite awful job was peeling onions in a pickle factory. I lasted two weeks. Somewhere in the decade of my twenties I began to reflect upon the mixture of wonderful and hurtful aspects of growing up as part of a rejected cultural group; at the same time Australia was beginning to embrace the rich diversity of a multicultural society. It was no longer shameful to like opera, to eat salami, and to look at life differently. The peculiar vegetables that only we had eaten now became fashionable: zucchini, radicchio, melanzine. 'New Australian' was displacing 'migrant' or 'reffo'. To have been brought up bilingual was an advantage instead of the shameful impurity it had been, and everybody was drinking cappucino instead of tea. Even wine appeared at meals, and, after the early horrors of Barossa Pearl and Cold Duck, actually became acceptable.

The years of shameful difference had left their marks. I was so deeply embedded in my yearning to be part of the dominant culture that I sought out Englishmen as partners, eventually marrying one. I was a daughter of the 1950's, a time in which women were trained to believe that power came through marriage. Even then, I couldn't quite get it right - he came from London working-class roots rather than the middle-class of my aspirations!

My thirties evoked the rebel once more as I had children and settled into suburbia. A long term interest in alternative or heterodox knowledge became a career path and I dwelt once more on the margins, this time of the helping professions, by being a successful astrologer. In the late seventies and early eighties such a career was definitely outré. The intriguing element for me was the clientele who came from the traditional helping professions. It occurred to me that my clients who were psychologists, social workers, doctors, and family therapists, in large part consulted me because of the non-pathologising stance of astrology. The act of being or seeing an astrologer may have been socially pathological, or at least deviant, but astrology itself was concerned with locating blame not within the person but within the cosmos.

While I did not know it at the time, taking up astrology as a career was in fact following an ancient family tradition. In exploring my own genealogy in some depth in the mid 90's, I made the discovery that I have gipsy heritage both on maternal and paternal lines of descent. Although it goes back four generations on one side and three on the other, perhaps it was inevitable that I spent some of my life exploring the bi-ways of this particular ethnicity.

And then I had a crisis of faith. Astrology is a time-based system and I made the devastating discovery that time, time-zones, and stellar time, were constructs, and constructs which served political masters at that! So I went back to university, yearning for credibility and respectability. I tried studying psychology but found my real niche in anthropology, the study of human(kind) - a discipline which demands its proponents learn to become outsiders while remaining insiders, experts on the Other whilst being high priests of the Self. It was in the anthropological battlefields of the mid-1980s that I began to realise that my early experience of being a liminar, living on the margins of the dominant culture, of imbibing the dominant discourse and rejecting the familial/cultural discourses of childhood, was a function of living within a racism so pervasive that it was invisible.

I remember an incident which exposed the struggle within me with painful clarity. I had written a paper and was giving a presentation of the ideas it pertained to ... I confided in the person who was to introduce me that I did not want my previous life as an astrologer revealed to an audience I hoped would become colleagues because I was 'trying to become respectable'. He thought this was a great joke, as well he might from his position as an entrenched professional male within the dominant discourse. He introduced me as 'Susi, who is trying to become respectable'. I writhed in misery at the betrayal; now I writhe at the poverty of what was then my ambition.

The university arena was the path I chose to climb into the rarefied heights of social acceptance. Even this revealed my non-Australian heritage. Only the children of migrants and the working-class were encouraged to see education as the means to social mobility in the decades of my childhood. To me, degrees meant (and still mean) the possibility of economic and social security, especially for a woman as she grows into rebellious middle age.

I am very aware that throughout those years there were basic necessities of life which were available to me but were denied to others. I had to fight cultural and historical gender norms to pursue an education to tertiary level in the 1960s but access to that education was not denied to me; we may have gone hungry from time to time but we had an extended family who could share resources - hunger was not a constant factor of our daily lives; we had good housing (Dad was a builder) and plain but adequate furniture, not a shanty or shed with a dirt floor to grow up in; medical attention was available and affordable; our clothing was limited but adequate (Nana made a pretty dress for each birthday and Christmas); a kind of cultural, pastoral care was offered through the Italian priests of the local teaching orders; and nobody came to take the children away. We were sufficiently part of 'European' history to be acknowledged as human, if not a lower caste of human, and not counted among the livestock (as Aboriginals were legally until the 1967 referendum). And, while as a woman I was often afraid of what men could do to me, I could walk down the street without being terrified for my life because of my skin colour.

If this sounds harsh, it is important to remember that racism is harsh and ugly and vicious, no matter what form it takes. When someone asks me why I work so passionately to oppose racism, I almost don't know what to say; life was difficult for me, but I can see how intolerable it is for others, especially people of colour.

I am very conscious of the impact of my early experience upon my life, and the painful working through of that experience, which has enabled me to see my childhood as a balance of idyllic and terrible. Even today I find myself pulled in opposing directions. No decision is simple or its outcome obvious. I agonise about doing a doctorate. On one hand I know that as a middle aged woman I need the credentials that a PhD will bring in order to be able to get a stable job. On the other, I am keenly aware that to invest my efforts in the patriarchal academic education system serves to buttress the significance of that world view. However, as I feel the distance growing from the margins (where I am at home) to the mainstream, I am faced with using the privilege of education responsibly so that others whose voices are not yet heard in academe can have an emissary, someone with a loud voice who can speak, not for, but on behalf of, those who are silenced.

The nineties have been a time of finding new stories in the ragbags of the old stories I had lived and framed along the way. Working more and more as a family therapist with a particular interest in people who live or have lived on the margins of the dominant culture, has become a joy and a delight for me. I am now proud of my heritage and have traced my ancestry on both sides. My father's family has been traced back to the family of Hannibal, Hanno and Hamilcar, and through three thousand years of European history. My mother's great-great-grandfather first came to Australia in 1827 in chains, a convict who settled near Jamberoo, and who had an Aboriginal as well as a white family. I'm still tracing my cousins. I suspect that most white Australians whose founding ancestors came here in the early years of settlement probably have Aboriginal cousins; it is very sad that it has taken us two hundred years to admit that we have hurt our own kin, and we are still doing it.

The reminder of those Sunday mornings decades ago brought to mind my Nonna, who died when I was eight. Nonna was a huge peasant women, of enormous strength, and a baker of exquisite foods. She had little English, my Italian was childish, but we would talk as I brushed her long silver hair. She used to pun on my name: I was called Marysue by Mum's family, Nonna used to call me 'Tiramisu' - pick-me-up. One day she told me something I shall never forget: 'Tiramisu', she said, 'be careful how you treat people - anyone could be your cousin'. Thanks Nonna.

P.S.

On Christmas morning I sat with my Italian father and my English partner, with my brothers, sisters and our children around us, and watched a video of The Barber of Seville. *This was probably the last time I'll share that opera with my Papa, who is growing frail. I will be feeling the spirited rhythms of Rossini's music and the impact of being an Italian Australian for the rest of my life.*

Acknowledgements

I would like to acknowledge these people, all of whom have contributed to my life, and therefore to this paper:

All my ancestors and relatives who have come from and who continue to be from a wide variety of people, whose colours, beliefs and ways of being have all enriched the existence of today's generation.

My friends and colleagues for being my friends and colleagues.

My father, Bert Bosa, for living a life of pain and displacement, while retaining dignity and courage; for teaching his children the importance of pride, honour and decorum, laughter and a love of fine food and music.

Aerinn Morgan

Aerinn Morgan has a background in nursing and teaching. She has worked in the area of mental health for twenty-four years. She lives in Adelaide with her family.

Mirror Mirror On The Wall

As a child, I learned that opinions were not for me. My family had audibly loud opinions with which I often disagreed but I dissented in silence. I felt unable to express myself adequately, and if I did succeed in fleetingly capturing some airspace, it only emphasised my feelings of being unheard and invisible. Having been recruited into invisibility early in my life, I learned that it held benefits for me only up to a certain point. Having had no experience at voicing opinions and taking a position, I was ill-equipped in adolescence to think for myself. This tension between invisibility and the desire to be heard (but also fear that I had nothing to say and that no-one would listen) led to delinquent behaviour, which I like to think of now as a huge protest against the invisibility, designed to keep me sane. These protests have continued into my adult life and, although probably now seen as socially acceptable, some still verge on 'shocking' to my family.

Without ever having had the words to express it, I knew from childhood that conversation and thoughts were never value-free. I knew well that I could only speak of certain things and in certain ways, and so I learned to listen. I was also well-coached in self-surveillance, and during my post-delinquent phase I excelled in finding out what I thought others wanted me to be, and being it. And so I aimlessly entered my twenties. People began asking me what was my philosophy of life? What did I value and believe in? Confronted with these questions, I frantically began to search for an 'ism' into which I could neatly fit. Existentialism, aetheism, feminism ... The list was endless and instead of finding an answer I found more dilemmas. Having to put forward and maintain a position meant that I had to disqualify others, but how could I know if I had chosen correctly?

I used to wonder why my otherwise loving, kind, generous and caring parents discounted or ignored my experiences. Now I ask myself different questions like, 'How did their experiences when they were growing up affect their beliefs about child-rearing?' Their intent did not always match their actions, but proof that they loved me was in abundance. Now that I am able to stop asking 'Why?', I am free to concentrate on the enquiry of how certain qualities in me were visible to them and how they had a harder time seeing others. And I am now more able to appreciate those positive qualities that they did nurture. In the same way my parents' experiences shaped their parenting, my experiences have shaped mine. Parenting is the hardest job I have ever undertaken and, although I congratulate myself on having wonderful children, I must also consider my own 'blind spots' in relation to them. I sometimes ask them how the way I have brought them up has affected them. They tell me it has had its difficulties. They are assertive and articulate but have sometimes felt different from other kids their own age. On the positive side, they tell me they feel listened to and respected. Knowing this is reassuring but does not relieve me of the responsibility to keep checking out their experience of my parenting. Knowing about the huge power inequalities between parents and their children, how can I be sure that I support a climate where they can say what they want to, rather than what they think I want to hear? As I well know from my own parents, love and good intentions are not always enough.

Having to think about accountability and how I can build it into whatever I do, is a responsibility that both frightens and relieves me. It frightens me because I might do something wrong, but it relieves me because I've been in many situations where I've had no-one to answer to, and I've been acutely aware of the potential dangers of relying totally on myself to do the 'right thing'. This has been an ongoing dilemma that has had huge implications for me in my work. I have worked in the psychiatric system, as a nurse, for twenty-four years. Accountability in nursing (and in all other professions that comprise the bulk of mental health workers) seems to have a very different meaning from the concept of accountability talked about by Kiwi Tamasese and others at The Family Centre in Lower Hutt, New Zealand. To me, accountability simply meant being able to justify my actions to my superiors, and then only when I had to. I knew that it felt uncomfortable to be in this position, but there was no way to tell anyone about my disquiet as I didn't fully comprehend it myself. I now realise that accountability is far more than simply having to report back to someone about my activities. Accountability is a tangible issue for me now and conforms more closely to The Family Centre's understanding of the term. This means that I am able to recognise the power imbalances in relationships and take steps to make myself answerable to those who have less power than me in any relationship in which I am involved. Putting this into practice is no simple matter, and it calls for far more than just the willingness to ask others about their experience of my actions. It also means creating a climate of safety for those in positions of less power so they feel comfortable enough to give feedback or criticism, and then being able to address the issues of concern and, most importantly, act on them.

I always used to think in terms of failure or success. I believed that if I was not good at something (as measured by acceptable standards that I saw set around me) then I should quit. I now know that evaluation is not an end in itself but an evolutionary process. It also goes beyond evaluating my own progress as a counsellor to evaluating the counselling process itself. And it goes well beyond looking for compliments or rewards from women I see. I've shifted to evaluating the process beyond me because if I concentrate on me or section off 'my progress' from 'the client's progress' then I feel like I'm missing the point.

At one stage I was concerned that my questions were too convoluted and difficult to answer, so I asked one woman if the questions were helpful or confusing. She said that they were difficult questions and she had to think about them, but the very fact that I asked them made her feel that I thought she was intelligent enough to answer them. Her answer surprised me and I had to think hard to understand why. I realised that when I had asked her that question, even though I genuinely wanted to know how the questions made her feel, I was really thinking about myself, regarding the questions simply as an indicator of how 'good' or 'bad' I was. Her answer re-focussed my attention onto our conversation and reminded me of my importance as a witness to her story. That question was a useful one for me to ask because it got me thinking about the difference between my experience of events and the other person's experience of those same events.

Allison Callie (1994) talks about accountability in her article on challenging heterosexual dominance. She described how witnessing her colleagues' attempts to 'get it right' was a very moving experience for her. However, she was also aware of how easy it was for them to become caught in their own discomfort rather than trying to respond to, or understand, her experience. I think this is what I fell into when I asked about how my questions were experienced. I am now beginning to see that accountability is about privileging the other person's experience over my own concerns of how I am being experienced by that person. The desire to respond to and understand other people's experiences has led me to a very different understanding of accountability.

A system's power goes far beyond the individuals within it. Many of us, as workers, have the best of intentions and work very hard to help people, but in our desire to help we often neglect to consult those whose experience is the most important. Although I never actually remember thinking about the meaning of this, when I look back, it must have seemed to clients that I thought I knew more about their experiences than they did. I referred people's experiences of hearing voices and feeling depressed back to my textbooks, rarely thinking to consult with them about their experience. I felt that I should always have the answers, but the knowledge that I didn't, and the assumption that others did, rattled my self-confidence. My training had led me to believe that I needed to maintain control and display competence in order to be helpful so, when I could not control others or even areas of my own life, I would feel powerless.

This dilemma between text-book knowledge and client's knowledge was only one of a number of conflicts that I discovered in my work. Sometimes advocating for clients meant going out on a limb and running the risk of having my judgement questioned by colleagues. This was a difficult thing for me to do as the system in which I worked never encouraged me to be totally confident about what I was doing. I had too many unanswered questions and no way of knowing how to ask them. It took me years to actually start asking those questions and even longer to find a voice for the answers. I was aware that being therapeutic meant that I was required to keep some distance between myself and the client so that I could maintain an objective stance. I could see that objectivity was an elusive goal, but I also knew that the degree to which I could be objective would be seen as a measure of my competence. I knew that I was in a position of power, in fact I was supposed to assume a position of power, but I never really felt powerful. More often I felt trapped into doing things against my better judgement.

Other dilemmas arose for me about gender. As a female nurse I was subject to gender inequalities and oppressive practices designed to keep me in my place. But as a nurse I was complicit in reproducing these oppressive practices with female patients. I saw many women whose experiences had similarities to my own. I could never talk about this openly because I feared being seen as too involved, which might leave me open to criticism. By remaining silent I succumbed to the power of the psychiatric system to pressure people to conform to their respective roles and consequently widened the gap between myself and my clients. I came to feel that I was acting a part. The only person who was not convinced by my portrayal was myself. I did not make up my role any more than other staff or clients made up theirs. We all conformed to the script even if, at times, our speeches sounded hollow.

In the last couple of years I have developed an understanding of my own experiences in the psychiatric system. I now have the words to express what was, for me, inexpressible before. I am now able to contextualise my experiences and to acknowledge what prompted so many mixed emotions. My work at a women's community health centre, this year, has shown me the absolute joy of working in a system that is not dominated by the psychiatric discourse. Other discourses predominate there which value people's own knowledges and experience. It is in the expression of these beliefs that I find a very comfortable fit. To reach this fit, I have had to challenge years of training: ideas like transference; not getting involved with clients; keeping a therapeutic distance; watching out for manipulative behaviours; looking for pathology; and displaying my expertise at all times.

All of these trainings took their toll on me and have affected me in different ways. Constantly searching for pathology was an exhausting and self-defeating quest. Releasing myself from the ideas and values of this training now allows me to reject the cynicism that I took on in those years. This has opened up a space for me to become more trusting of others. It also has enabled me to begin to trust my own judgement.

One of the many things that I have learned is that I gain and grow from each encounter that I have with people who consult me. Some gains are larger than others, but it has been a very useful way to reflect on my practice because it makes me think about the contributions that we both make to the session.

One client who helped me understand this, Elizabeth, first came to see me talking rapidly, and it seemed to me at the time that I was having trouble understanding what she was trying to say. She looked tired and tense. A friend of Elizabeth's had suggested to her that she would benefit from learning to become more assertive. Over many sessions she told and re-told her story, sometimes repeating parts, but always filling out and adding on so that the story became very rich and intricate. Many times I wondered what was going on. It appeared that, in telling her story and having me as an audience, something was happening. I knew validation was extremely important, but there seemed to be more going on than that. The process itself seemed alive, but I seemed unable to fully comprehend and articulate what was occurring. Going back to Barbara Meyerhoff's work helped me to appreciate the process better.

Elizabeth had been forced, by circumstances, to live outside of Australia for twenty years. She had been cut off from her family, her friends and her culture. These experiences, that were so important, she had tried to keep alive in herself without any outside support. On her return to Australia she felt herself to be an outsider in her own birthplace. At first she lived in the country but then returned to the city after she left her marriage. Understandably, such changes had consumed much of her energy, and it was some time before she could sustain the hard work required to reclaim what she had lost. I wondered if she too was struggling to make sense of what had happened to her and to find some meaning in her experiences.

Each time we sat together I wondered, 'Am I helping?', and, 'If only I had more skills', and yet each time I felt that something almost imperceptible was changing, although it was nothing that I could articulate. Meyerhoff (1980, p.112) says that the need to retell a story is seldom to change things or to obtain repentance. She says: *It is to forge a link with the listener, to retain one's past, to find evidence of sense, above all it is an assertion of an unextinguished presence.* I felt very much that I was privileged in bearing witness to this testimony of 'unextinguished presence'. As the weeks went by I watched Elizabeth become more confident and assertive.

We continue to meet. She is still coping with some extremely difficult issues in her life, and I often wonder if her strength and courage are as visible to her as they are to me. I have gained a lot from our association because she also acted as a witness for me. She was a witness to my growing faith in these new ways of working. It was hard for me to always have this faith because I felt, at times, that I might be letting her down.

Elizabeth helped me to develop a space for 'not knowing', for which I am very grateful, and it is something that I have been able to take into my work with other women.

Reflecting on these gains is very sustaining. Without this process I can fall into thinking that I am constantly giving. This can lead to burnout, which happened to me over the past couple of years. Relationships with my family and friends suffered. I had experienced what, then, I interpreted to be a lack of care and compassion towards the people I love the most. In retrospect, I understand that I was giving more than I was receiving, and the result was a feeling of burnout. Narrative therapy has re-acquainted me with my feelings of compassion and acutely attuned me to the need to look after myself as a way of ensuring that those negative feelings of self-blame do not recur. Being in tune with the way the work affects me and how I gain from these exchanges is only one of a growing number of self-care strategies. The ability to reflect on what I gain from sessions not only enables me to seek help when I need it, but also helps me to connect more fully with my feelings of compassion, empathy and caring. Reconnecting with these feelings is not only a source of joy for me in that it enriches my life, but also aids my development as a counsellor.

The journey to finding my own voice has been a slow one. It has involved times of moving ahead and feeling good about myself, and times when I feel that any ground I may have gained has been lost. I remind myself that the journey itself is as important, if not more so, than the destination. I am freer now to ask questions, and, if I find that I still have to struggle with the answers, then at least I feel I am in a more comfortable space to be able to hear them.

References

Callie, Alison, 1994:
    'Pain, hope and heterosexual dominance.' *Dulwich Centre Newsletter*, 2&3.
Meyerhoff, Barbara, 1980:
    Life History Among the Elderly: Performance, visibility and re-membering.
Tamasese, Kiwi & Waldegrave, Charles, 1993:
    'Cultural and gender accountability in the "Just Therapy" approach.' *Journal of Feminist Family Therapy*, 5(2).

Acknowledgements

My Grandmother died when I was very young and so I never really knew her. I am told that she was a 'stubborn' woman. I would like to thank her for passing on to my mother her 'stubbornness' which has given me the same strength and determination that I have witnessed in her over the years. I now witness these qualities in my sons.

I thank my father for my early training in pragmatism, so that, when my head was in the clouds, at least my feet were always firmly on the ground. I thank them both for their patience, love, sense of humour and support throughout my life. They have earned my utmost love, respect and admiration.

Sue Jackson

Sue works predominantly in private practice in Melbourne. She is a heterosexual woman and mother of 3 wonderful children. Sue has worked in England and Australia as a family, individual and couples therapist and trainer since 1975. Sue's current areas of interest include HIV/AIDS, gay and lesbian relationship counselling, and body image in women.

Another Fortunate Life

A good part of being alive is staying alive on purpose.
(William Wharton, 1984)

This seems to me to be one of the fundamental issues of life and therapy both. It is also one of the main reasons why I was so attracted to being a therapist and what keeps me here. So many of us live half-lives or are preoccupied with issues which deplete our resources and give us very little joy. Often it takes a crisis for us to reflect on our lives and to adjust our priorities accordingly. How wonderful to live each day truly as if it was your last, to experience and savour moments fully. One of the joys of therapeutic work is that all day long I am exposed to people who are wrestling with highly charged issues and surprising themselves with their strength and creativity. In this rich context it is much harder to lose sight of the preciousness of life. It also gives additional validity to my own struggles to live an aware and meaningful life because many of the people I see are engaged in the same process. I believe that we are best positioned to have creative conversations - for me the essence of therapy - when our minds and hearts are open to new possibilities for ourselves as well as for our clients. In that sense my own personal journey both informs and is informed by the therapeutic relationships of which I am a part. As Wharton puts it, in speaking of an artist, the main protagonist in his book:

> *I want to paint everybody not so much the way they look but the way they are to me. I'm the lowest common denominator, the something that's in all of them. It's the way they are in this book, all partly me. And me, I'm partly them, the way they want me to be. The people and objects in this world only SEEM separate. In the big picture we're all the same thing, one greater being.*

Fundamentally it feels such a privilege to spend my days talking to people who are struggling to live meaningful lives, and to be party to their most intimate dreams and hopes.

Working in the area of HIV/AIDS, as I have for about ten years now, has had an enormous impact on my own life. I hardly know where to begin to describe some of the many things I have learned from associating with people with the virus and AIDS, their partners, families (of origin, procreation and choice), and the carers who support them.

Balance

People who are daily confronted with their mortality have often shed preoccupations which constrain the rest of us, and have made active choices about how to spend their remaining time most productively. For them, balance is often a key issue and one which is hard to achieve in mainstream society where the work ethic still predominates. In fact, an increasing number of couples seem to be presenting to me with issues that essentially involve them allowing an insufficiency of time to keep their relationships healthy and intimate in nature. Their therapy session may be the first opportunity they have had for an in-depth conversation since the last time we met! Simply, if you do not spend time together you lose each other. For employed people in our society, time has become the greatest luxury, and workplace cultures often compound this problem by making it difficult for individuals to privilege time with their partners and families. Once HIV enters a person's life, decisions about workload, stress and lifestyle become of paramount importance. It is interesting to see the speed and even enthusiasm with which people often make decisions to curtail or cease careers which previously seemed crucial to their sense of well-being and identity.

Paradoxically, I have learned that to keep myself available at an emotional level for my clients requires that I place other aspects of my life as a high priority. For a start I need time for lunch! I raise that because I am reminded of a conversation I had recently on that very topic with my colleagues in the HIV team. I was boasting that I had finally taken action and had blocked out time for lunch every day from then on in my diary. One of my colleagues replied: 'That's fine, but how will your clients feel about you talking with your mouth full?'

Pressures of work will always make it supremely difficult for us to treat ourselves as well as we encourage others to treat themselves. I have finally learned (I hope) that essentials for me include time for my children and partner, for family and friends, for creativity, for fun and play, for exercise and, most importantly, time alone for reflection and contemplation - without this I am inclined to merely amass an increasing number of experiences but quickly become overwhelmed, stressed and not fully present to the next experience in which I am involved. So, to live an aware life, I believe, necessitates continuously making choices about what to shed. This in turn involves an ongoing process of examination of one's priorities. Perhaps there is a developmental congruence to this. Earlier in life is like a fishing expedition. It is good to cast your net widely to see what you might catch. Perhaps in midlife it is more appropriate to make choices to discard some areas for the pleasure of going deeper in others. People who are facing imminent death make these decisions all the time and often report the relief involved in letting go of some of their former preoccupations. Some of the things they do not let go of fascinate me too - humour and vanity to mention just two - but more of that later.

Love

A continuing drawcard for me as a therapist is the constant exposure to the lived power of love, and especially to peoples' great capacity to entirely transform themselves in that cause.

I am reminded of Jean, a recent client, very young, very innocent about life, who discovered six years into a relationship that her partner was infected when he developed AIDS-related symptoms. Jean, who is shy, somewhat unassuming, and sometimes stutters when stressed, went into bat fearlessly for her partner on many occasions, often with high-status members of the medical establishment. It was wonderful to see her delight in the discovery of her ability to be a David to their Goliath! Her partner, John, desperately wanted to die at home, partly because he was afraid of hospitals, and also because, as he became sicker, he developed a great dependency on Jean and could not bear to have her out of his sight. Jean had had no prior nursing experience and yet, in her determination to help John achieve his goal, she managed to learn procedures whose descriptions were even harrowing to me. She gave him injections, changed his bedding continually, assisted him at every intimate level, and managed to remain positive and matter of fact most of the time.

Jean and John had met through a snooker club and were both competent, competition-standard players. Not long before John died, Jean surprised him by organising a party for him at their old club. She had been somewhat nervous about this in advance because she had been very open about his diagnosis. Subsequently Jean described with utter delight the wonderful reception his fellow players gave John. It was great to share her pleasure in this and her realisation that she had accessed yet another unexpected facet of herself in making such an event possible.

A few months before John died, Jean gave up work outside the home and devoted herself entirely to John's care. Jean's family lives interstate and, although she received considerable professional support, much of the time she nursed him alone. Before he became ill, John, who was somewhat older than Jean and more streetwise, had been the decision-maker and the more assertive partner. However, as his condition worsened their roles reversed. To assist his comfort and in hopes of improving his condition, Jean was able when necessary to become very firm with John, sometimes insisting that he eat and take his medication, even when she felt she was being cruel.

The last month was extremely difficult, with broken nights, little sleep, and Jean's terror that she would awake one morning to find John dead beside her. When I alluded to this fact in one session, Jean commented: 'But it has never before been so wonderful between us. We have never been closer. It is just so good to have this special time to be together.' Such is the power of love!

Humour

One of the main reasons I have continued to work in the area of HIV/AIDS is that the people are so much fun!

Let me recount some of the experiences of a man I met just last week. I will call him Adam. Adam has known his positive diagnosis for some years and has already outlived what he felt was his death sentence. He said that one of the things he finds most irritating is that when he is in hospital well-meaning staff often greet him with: 'And how are *we* today?' He said he is often tempted to reply: 'Who do you mean - my virus and I?'

Another odd response is that when people, even relative strangers, want to demonstrate support they tend to hug him and 'burp' him at the same time. He finds it difficult to know how to respond to this appropriately!

Adam also related how, soon after his diagnosis, he took a cruise to see the world - a not uncommon response to a positive diagnosis. When on board, he realised that the ship provided a perfect opportunity to kill himself. He went up to the highest deck and jumped. At that very moment the ship listed, and instead of ending up in the sea he landed on the deck below. The ship's crew were so worried that it was the movement of the ship that had caused his fall that he scored a free world cruise!

Adam described how, even though his elderly parents knew he was gay, they managed never to refer to this fact directly. Adam used to be a flight attendant and as such he often stayed with his parents between flights. One evening he had just packed his bag preparatory to returning to work. As a surprise his mother opened his bag to pack a fruit(!) cake she had baked. In pride of place in the bag were his new, bright red patent leather stiletto heels. Her only response was to comment to him later in the car: 'They won't fit, you know!'

I have learned that people cannot long survive with an undiluted diet of tragedy. Therefore tragedy and absurdity make natural bedfellows. I believe that marginalised groups have long known this. Hence working with service users and service providers who are predominantly gay and lesbian means that humour and laughter is part of our staple fare.

There is quite a literature on the use of humour by marginalised groups. We have also discussed this phenomenon in the HIV team. Some of the ideas which emerged included the fact that humour often works because of the odd juxtaposition of familiar events or propositions, and people who are not part of the dominant culture are better positioned to see the humorous side of things. In other words, gay people, with their metaperspective on mainstream society, having struggled to find their own niche, within or without, are inclined to have a more unconventional view, and unconventional views more readily spawn humour. My gay colleagues suggested that humour has been used to unite the gay community, for protest, and also to establish a unique identity. The comment was also made that humour which is self-directed can anticipate prospective barbs and, by making them part of the humorist's armoury, reduce the capacity to wound. Whatever the reasons, what often emerges are wonderful demonstrations of the courage, dignity and resilience of the human spirit.

A final example from a client who has since died demonstrates for me how people can display immense courage in extremes. Andrew had recently begun treatment for CMV, an HIV-related disorder of the eyes, which if untreated leads to blindness. To counteract this condition necessitates the extensive use of IV drips several times a week indefinitely. One side-effect of this condition is spots in front of the eyes. Andrew had been filling in the therapist on this condition and the treatment. The therapist, who was quite upset on his client's behalf, tried to commiserate with him. Andrew's response was: 'Don't fret. You look great in spots!'

Creativity

I have become increasingly aware of how much human distress is caused by the damming up of creative energies - which in our current society have not been rewarded in the same way as have more conventionally 'useful' talents. Routinely questioning people about their creative outlets, and more particularly about those dreams they may have had earlier in life and felt the need to bury, has proved incredibly fruitful. I have learned to do this because of the transformation that committing oneself to a creative direction can render in people's lives.

In this context I would like to talk about Adrian, a highly intelligent, articulate man, with a most expressive face and wonderful saturnine eyebrows. Adrian presented as severely depressed with little vitality and an angry, cynical approach to life. He had made a very serious suicide attempt in the not-too-distant past, and felt that he was a worthless person who would be better off dead. He said that he had felt this way for the last thirty of his thirty-five years. Adrian, whose father has an alcohol problem, reported using both alcohol and marijuana heavily.

Adrian had been an art student some fifteen years earlier and had subsequently successfully completed a master's degree in art history. When I first met him he was struggling to hold down a job which he described as 'utterly soul-destroying' in the public service. He was bitterly unhappy but as he had had a prolonged period of unemployment after completing his higher degree, he felt that he had no option but to stay put. In one of our sessions, Adrian confessed, somewhat hesitantly, that he had always wanted to be a painter. I responded by saying that, as he seemed to me to be an unconventional person, I could understand how that ambition would be very consistent for him. Subsequently he has said that my simple comment that he seemed an unconventional person had a huge impact on him. Initially he took on voluntary work in two art galleries. Soon afterwards he resigned from his job and committed himself to a life as a painter.

I am still seeing Adrian but now he brings his beautiful paintings to show me. So far he has only displayed his pictures to artist friends but is preparing to approach a gallery owner soon. Nowadays he is completely different: confident, optimistic, happy with his lot and the direction his life is taking. In fact, he is utterly transformed and it is wonderful to see.

An aside - but another important thing I was reminded of by Adrian's experience - is that frequently I have needed to give up something or to leave space in my life in order to see what new opportunities might present. When life is full of activity, wonderful possibilities probably pass us by without our having the emotional space to recognise their potential. Adrian is absolutely sure that, had he kept to the safe option and continued to work at his conventional job, he would never have realised his life's ambition to be a painter.

Spirituality

So many of the people I meet nowadays seem to have a rich and developing spiritual dimension in their lives. I also notice that, as my own interest in this area increases, many people choose to tell me stories that seem to make little sense in rational terms yet make great sense at other levels. They will often preface these stories with comments such as: 'You'll probably think I'm crazy, but I would like to tell you something'. Here is one example.

A young woman client told me a strange story. Her father, who lives in San Francisco, had a brain haemorrhage. His wife and four children flew in from around the globe and spent a very long night clustered around his bed. Happily, he survived and later recovered. At dawn my client, exhausted, jet-lagged, and more than a little dishevelled, decided to take a walk down to Fisherman's Wharf. As she emerged from the hospital she was surrounded by a large group of cats. She checked her handbag to ensure that she had not inadvertently picked up some raw meat or something equally enticing in her travels. Reassured on that score, she expected the cats to disperse. In fact they followed her on her walk, an entourage she said she found strangely comforting. One of my other clients, in an entirely different context, told me how she believes that cats have a heightened awareness of human emotions!

Something that fascinates me is the uncanny way in which sometimes my clients' lives and my own seem to intersect - I have dubbed it cosmic synchronicity. Why, when I was in the throes of my own separation, but before it was public knowledge, did so many of my clients present with issues of separation? When I am worried about money, why do financial concerns often seem to be the preoccupation of the people I see? Is it merely coincidence, like when you are pregnant and the streets seem full of women in the same condition? I prefer to believe that there are aspects of the therapeutic relationship which are not entirely amenable to verbal explanation. For example, there are times when a client is talking and I have an image, a feeling or an association, which seems to come from nowhere but which is often incredibly apposite. My increasing comfort with these ideas has been deeply influenced by the many people with whom I work who themselves are living with high levels of uncertainty in their lives and who have embraced a rich spiritual dimension.

Certainly in this whole domain of spirituality I am left with many questions and few answers - a not uncomfortable position in which to be.

Meaning

In the last couple of years my practice has been greatly influenced by Viktor Frankl's *Man's Search for Meaning*, a book which the author wrote as a result of his experiences as a prisoner in Auschwitz. Frankl was a psychiatrist who utilised his analytical skills extensively during his incarceration. Essentially he felt that people, even in such extreme conditions as a concentration camp, struggle to find meaning in their lives. Developing purpose and meaning in life is always restorative and sometimes can even assist people to survive in circumstances where death would seem much the easier option.

Frankl concluded that most people find meaning primarily via three sources. Love is the first. Frankl described most poignantly the comfort he experienced in his ability to evoke his wife's presence and converse with her (even though tragically, and unknown to him, she was already dead). Jean, who I mentioned earlier, is one example of the many people I have known who have made meaning of their life through love.

Frankl's second source of meaning is via projects and actions which are worthy and by means of which people can transcend their own individual concerns and the limitations of the moment. There were many examples cited in the book of inmates demonstrating such behaviour. One that I recall vividly was of an old hand who risked terrible reprisals to brief new arrivals on behaviours that were likely to assist their survival, for example shaving to keep up a semblance of fitness for work. In the area in which I work, infected and affected people who are heavily represented in care teams for people with AIDS and such organisations as PLWHA (People Living with HIV and AIDS) often make the point that assisting others enables them to keep their own problems in perspective. It can also enhance their sense of making a contribution, of leaving a legacy and, particularly for people with no children, it can give them a sense of continuity.

Thirdly, Frankl observed that many people were able to experience their lives as meaningful through their endurance and stoicism with regard to suffering. This is something which never ceases to fill me with wonder and admiration when working with terminally ill people.

I have found over time that there are in fact many ways in which people make meaning of their lives, and their creativity in this regard is one of the aspects of therapeutic work that I find most fascinating.

I recall an older couple I saw quite a few years ago who have stayed in my memory. Frank and Alice were in their mid 60s. I had met them because one of their children had received a diagnosis of schizophrenia and had a recurrent problem with self-mutilation. I saw the whole family together for some time until their daughter's problems had improved to the extent that the parents felt freed up to pursue some of their own interests.

Alice and Frank had had a somewhat conventional relationship where he was the provider, who rarely intruded into Alice's domain, the kitchen. Alice had been totally devoted to household duties and the raising of their four children. Alice described how in many ways the last twenty years had felt like a long sleep. However, she did not want Prince Charming to awaken her with a kiss. She wanted to do that for herself! Alice was a deeply religious woman, who had been sustained through many troubles by her religious faith. Even though she had never worked outside the home nor pursued any tertiary education, she decided to embark on a degree in divinity. To facilitate her studies, she borrowed a friend's caravan and parked it in the backyard. She bought, and taught herself how to operate, a computer, which she moved into the caravan. To a large degree Frank took over the household chores.

I can still remember vividly our final session where the couple related this revolution in their domestic routine and their lives. Frank, who still seemed a little bewildered at the extent and speed of the changes, was simultaneously immensely proud of his wife and amazed at her new-found abilities. Alice commented that, while the degree of her husband's flexibility was something of a surprise, she had always suspected its existence. And Alice herself - well, I can only describe her as being totally in love with her new life. She detailed the thrill of tutorials, the stimulation of new ideas and opportunities for intellectual debate in an area which captivated her interest. Alice was well and truly awake!

Why do I remember this so vividly? I think because I felt so heartened by the realisation that, through love of another and faith in oneself, it is never too late to find meaning in life and to realise your dreams.

Another way in which many people make meaning in their lives is by returning to nature. One example of the restorative potential of this course will suffice.

I was seeing a young woman who was deeply troubled. Kerry had long-standing communication difficulties with both her parents and her brother. She had totally lost faith in her career choice. She felt incredibly isolated. What brought Kerry into therapy was that one night she was looking out her front door at dusk when she observed a young man poised uncertainly on the train platform opposite her flat. She watched him with disquiet and was on the point of calling out when he threw himself under a passing train. This absolutely shattered Kerry and made her doubt the point of proceeding with her own life. Thoughts of suicide consumed her waking hours and her dreams. I was deeply concerned that she might take her own life.

During a discussion of the things that she found nurturing, Kerry highlighted the significance of the bush, outdoor activities in general, and rock-climbing in particular, as being fundamental to her sense of well-being. But because of a gruelling work and study schedule she had not been rock-climbing for more than eighteen months. When next we met she seemed quite transformed. Kerry had responded to an invitation from an old friend to go rock-climbing. She described with great joy the thrill of again sleeping under the stars. She was especially heartened by the experience she had when she attempted her first climb. She had felt very nervous and when she tried to remember how to climb this had made her feel worse. Then she decided to let her body remember for her. She balanced herself, stopped thinking, and allowed her limbs to find their natural momentum. As a result she had a most enjoyable climb. She found it extremely comforting to realise that she had skills and knowledge which did not need to be mediated by a brain already in overload. Kerry was quite sure that it was as a result of the calmness and comfort she experienced in re-immersing herself in nature that she had begun to redevelop this trust in her intuitive side and bodily wisdom, capacities which she believed might well pull her through this particularly tough time in her life.

I am inclined to agree with Frankl that the struggle to make meaning of one's life is almost a universal phenomenon. Although it presents in numerous different guises, it is frequently the fundamental issue with which our clients are wrestling. However, it is important to contextualise this experience, to note that issues such as widespread unemployment, changing work patterns, and the increasing gulf between the rich and the poor in our society, add a particularly difficult dimension to this struggle for many people in this last decade of the millennium.

Conclusion

I spend much time talking to colleagues about the fascinating things I am learning from my clients, and so it has been wonderful to have this opportunity to share some of these recollections with a wider audience. Recently I was asked to present at a workshop called 'Eating Awareness and Body Image'. As I have been working and presenting in this area for a decade, I decided to review my personal practice in preparation. It was astounding to find that, although the seeds of my current practice were in evidence ten years ago, my present orientation is entirely different. The wisdom that I have gleaned from my clients has been fundamental in this shift. It is intriguing to think that were I compiling this piece a year or two hence it would be likely to be quite different. Such is the richness of the experiences available to a therapist.

References

Frankl, V. 1984:
  Man's Search for Meaning. New York: Touchstone.
Wharton, W. 1984:
  Scumbler. New York: Alfred A Knopf.

Acknowledgements

Acknowledgement to A.B. Facy, whose story of his life in Australia earlier this century is most inspiring.

I would also like to acknowledge Peter McIville for his encouragement, generous support and helpful criticism throughout the writing of this paper.

Marie Tudor

Marie is a medical practitioner and counsellor working in private practice in Adelaide. Her work, which is predominantly with people with sexual and relationship concerns, is informed by narrative and feminist ideas. She lives in the Adelaide Hills with her partner, Con, and their two children, James and Michael.

Sexual Therapy Encounters Of The Narrative Kind

Several years ago I made a decision to move away from my general medical practice work. This marked my quest to find work that I loved, rather than something I did out of habit or a sense of duty. I took this step at a time when 'looking after others' had taken over my life - to the point of not knowing what I would like in life for myself, even when I was encouraged to dream about what this might be.

Some months into my quest I took up the opportunity to do some sexual counselling within my role as a medical practitioner in a family medicine clinic. My previous medical training had prepared me well for yet another 'learn-on-the-job' position. The authority conferred upon and accepted by me as a doctor, helped me to develop the courage and willingness to throw myself into a field that I had generally left to more experienced colleagues.

However, the same medical training environment had *also* nurtured self-doubt. Textbook knowledge and performance had been expected, despite our trainee status and our enormously variable caseload. This promoted competition between colleagues, leaving little room for collaboration, and contributed to one's striving to know *all*, to be the expert in one's designated area. The cost was enormous. I had to be on constant guard - a mistake could cost a life. The seriousness of *this* responsibility was accepted without question. What was difficult yet tolerated was the attitudes of many of the senior staff whose role it was to support those working 'under them'. The lack of help at times of crisis, emergency, and uncertainty, added to a feeling of burden in what I thought should be an exciting career.

During the years following the hospital training I worked in general medical practices. Although my work was well regarded by my colleagues and patients, I rarely had a sense of being good enough. A training adviser, commenting on my work as a general practitioner, described me as 'a pig in mud'! Hearing this response felt strange; there seemed to be a disparity between the outsider's view of my work and my internal sense of worth and fulfilment. The hangover of trainee self-doubt revealed its continuing effects through a competence-confidence struggle within me at work. The main strategy I employed to overcome these feelings of self-doubt was to dedicate more time to my patients, more time to continued education, and more time to worrying about the many daily medical decisions.

There were days when I loved the family doctor role, when I felt I was making a difference in people's lives. There were usually days when my work extended beyond the usual technical skills required of me - when I was able to offer more than recounted knowledge and medical advice. However, the time required to support people with compassion and understanding usually put me in a time-pressured situation, which ultimately added to the stress of the job.

My striving for excellence filtered into the counselling I did within general practice. When people continued to suffer, feel confused, or stuck in their dilemmas or suffering, I revisited the feelings of doubt in my abilities, asking myself where *I* was going wrong. The cost of my training in over-acceptance of responsibility and the desire to 'fix' people's problems was the eventual diversion of much of my energy away from self-care and enjoyment of personal and family pursuits.

My previous medical training and experience had not prepared me to answer the many questions that were emerging as I took up this new counselling role and began to work with a variety of people with sexual concerns:

- How am I qualified to help people with their sex lives?
- How do I know that my 'hypothesis' about the couple's sexual problem is 'correct'?
- What *don't* I know that I *should* know?
- How do I learn at a rate that keeps up with my clients' needs?
- How responsible am *I* if the couple do not find their 'problem' improving?
- How do I best address past childhood sexual abuse?
- How do I view sexual concerns within a gay or lesbian relationship?

My earlier apprentice-style work in this field was composed of a mix of ideas from sex therapists of the 1970s and 1980s (eg. Masters and Johnson, Helen Singer Kaplan and J. LoPiccolo) and the latest popular psychology readings.

I was keen to learn protocols for each sexual 'problem', thinking that time would give me the experience I needed to feel more comfortable in this work. Information sheets on 'depression' were available to hand to people to take home for comparison with their own symptoms; antidepressants were often prescribed for men with erectile difficulties and for the person with the least sexual desire (quite a task for me as a conservative prescriber). I rapidly learnt to record relaxation tapes during sessions for the 'symptomatic' client (i.e. the one with erectile difficulties or vaginal muscle spasm) to take home. This included my version of a successful sexual encounter for the client, incorporating several situational details specific to their needs. (I received very little negative feedback when I asked people what the experience was like - but what level of courage would it take to do this?!!) I instructed the men with ejaculatory or erectile difficulties to do the 'Masturbation Exercises'. I found myself forever seeking and collecting readily available phallic office objects for demonstration of these exercises(!!), which included the squeeze technique to delay ejaculation. These men were provided with a chart to fill in the duration they were managing to masturbate before squeezing. They were also provided with *Penthouse* magazines, if they wished, to help them get into the mood. Most people were given firm instructions not to have intercourse and to do my prescribed homework exercises. I sent people home with educational and R-rated movies of their choice - a number of which I hadn't seen myself - and self-help books or novels I hadn't had time to read.

I employed these commonly accepted methods in a learn-as-you-go fashion, trusting that people's sexual problems would improve. Whilst some of the people overcame their sexual difficulties, others complained that they weren't getting anywhere, and felt I was focussing on the wrong issues. When people's specific performance goals were not being met, criticism and complaints of the effectiveness of my work found their way into our conversations. I became drawn into self-blaming thoughts: 'If only I had more experience, they would improve'. I was caught up with my clients in a belief that they would resolve their problems if only I gave enough of the right advice and counselling. I suspected that there were some important gaps in my knowledge, yet, at the same time, I questioned if more experience with this behavioural approach would really provide me with the skills needed to help the people who were consulting me.

Several months into this new vocation, I enrolled in a training course which focussed on a more social constructionist perspective rather than on behavioural techniques. This resulted in a broadening of my view in this work. The environment of enquiry nurtured my growing concerns about my role as 'educator' or 'expert' in which I was prescribing, proscribing and taking for granted certain 'normative' ideas around sexual practices.

My ways of listening and viewing the problems I saw each day began to change, as did the sorts of questions I began to formulate for myself and those who consulted me. These included:
- What shapes our ideas and beliefs about sexuality?
- What roles do our society, family, partners, education and the media play?
- Who decides what the nature of the sexual problem is and *who* 'has it'?
- Are these beliefs and ideas about sexuality and sexual practices ones that enrich our lives and relationships?
- Are there other ways of being sexual and addressing sexual concerns that may be more suitable for our lives?
- What might prevent us from exploring these other ways?
- What if we didn't believe all that we presently do about our own or others'

sexuality?

- What difference would that make to our experience of our sexuality and to our lives?

Using a social constructionist approach and narrative therapy ideas, I entered into conversations more frequently with people to explore their beliefs, understandings, hopes and expectations for their relationships, intimacy and sexuality. I became more aware of the effects of patriarchal notions and beliefs on people's relationships, and discovered previously hidden cultural and political forces that shape peoples' experiences of their sexuality. I examined, together with people who consulted me, the various discourses that informed their stories about their intimate relationships and sexuality, using externalising conversations. I was keen to explore other discourses that could contribute to alternative stories of their sexual experiences, their relationships and their lives. This shift from a modernist 'expert' position to one of curiosity about the knowledges of those who sought help was enormously challenging, yet exhilarating.

As I continued my journey into the world of narrative therapy, I also noticed changes occurring in my own life. I began questioning the origins of my feelings of self-doubt and over-responsibility in terms of my training as 'a good and helpful girl'. I recalled how I had learnt to defer to men's demands to avoid unpleasantness. I have no lingering childhood regrets or a need to blame others - I am just more aware of the greater invitation open to girls and women in our society to feel responsible for others' needs to the exclusion of their own.

My discovery of a more balanced sense of responsibility came through different ways I found to value and view myself. I began to recall the moments of encouragement from mentors who noticed qualities in me that were given less priority by other colleagues. A consultant on the physical medicine ward had said, as his parting comment to me, 'You're a "people person" Marie. I hope you choose a field where you will continue to work with people'. The memory of these words has provided a counter-voice to my internal authority-voice and has been a support to me during moments of resurfacing self-doubt.

Valuing my skills and career-path now in terms of my commitments and personal qualities (which I believe include the love, support, compassion and respect I am able to offer people) has led to more self-respect and self-nurturing ways. This has resulted in a sustained energy and enthusiasm for the possibilities in my work and life, and leaves little space now for self-doubt. My guess is that, if I were to return to general practice work now with this growing sense of self-worth, I would be less vulnerable to 'burnout'.

The authority and expert role was one that I was still playing at the outset of my sexual counselling work. This was the way I had previously learnt to appear credible in the face of inexperience, but the consequence for me was that feelings of responsibility and self-doubt returned. It was not until I developed a style of work that broke away from the authority role that I felt a freedom and lightness in my work that I thought was previously unattainable. I moved away from advice-giving toward hearing people's own hopes and understandings of how they could draw upon their own expertise. This transition also occurred on a personal level for me. I found myself questioning others' expectations of the way I should live. I decided to refrain from the practice of 'knowing' what was best for others - whether that was my partner, my children or friends. With this shift away from over-responsibility came an immense happiness and energy and a sense of my world opening up before me. I had only ever experienced these feelings during a time of travel through India in 1983. This time marked the completion of exams and was a time of discovery of a new world - a freedom from the seriousness that dominated my life at home. My return to Australia coincided with a dissipation of much of this sense of freedom and happiness. I just assumed that these feelings were only attainable on vacation, their intensity most likely being proportional to the distance from home! However, when I began to re-experience this happiness and sense of freedom for sustained periods in my counselling work (even whilst dealing with people's serious life concerns), it dawned on me that I had discovered a way of working that fulfilled my quest - without yearning for the next holiday escape!

My journey into narrative therapy over the last few years has been interwoven with my personal and professional journey away from self-doubt in the face of authority - a doubt that has often led me to the fear of being wrong. However, the preparedness to be open to doubt and to being wrong is, I now understand, at the heart of accountability to the people who consult me. It is not surprising to me, therefore, that I have at times confused these two doubts.

An ongoing project for me is to welcome and practice this new feeling of doubt which allows me an awareness of other options in my work and life generally. If feelings of burden or responsibility or the internal authoritarian voice return to create the old self-doubt, I hope that these will alert me to question the ways I am working - to ensure that the 'fix-it role' does not return.

Although exciting, this vocation change has not been easy. The greatest challenge for me has been to find ways of coping with the 'booming voices' in my work. These voices usually (although not always) take the form of men's frustration and anger; anger about their partners' lack of desire for sex or failure to agree with their opinions, or frustration with themselves and their feelings of sexual inadequacy. The booming voices may also surface when I decline to enter into conversations where men blame their partner. When these booming voices bombard me, they tend to press the 'replay' button on other authoritative voices I have also experienced in my life. The effects of this on my manner include: self-doubt ('He must know best'); confusion; paralysis of thoughts; submission; politeness; and attempts at placation. At times I have even found myself matching their authoritative booming voices, as I recall doing at times in my role as a doctor. This approach only seems to turn *up* the volume of all the voices so that there is no room to hear anything!

Instead, I have begun to talk with men about the impact of their ways of talking on me. ('What effect do you think this way of talking has on me in my conversations with you?') I may then follow with questions such as:

- Do you think this way of talking will help or undermine your hopes for this session?
- Does this way of talking surface in your everyday life, or does this only occur in this counselling context? How would you explain this?
- Would your partner ever hear you talking in this (booming/authoritative) way?
- What effect do you think this would have on her/him if s/he experienced your voice as authoritative?
- Does this way of talking help you and your partner with your concerns, or do you think it might escalate them?
- How did you develop this style of communication?
- Has this way of communicating always suited you *and* your partner, or have there been some disadvantages with it?
- If this is not your preferred way of communicating, how do you think you may have been drawn into this way?
- Have there been other ways of communicating that have allowed more open discussions with your partner about your concerns?

These types of questions have resulted in some more helpful conversations with men and have helped me reduce the volume of booming voices in my work.

I have been experimenting with ways of working with people who expect me, as a doctor, to take the expert position and provide answers. I am continuing to learn ways of declining these invitations to make people's decisions for them. I am learning to decline the self-invitation to feel a failure or useless if people feel their relationship is not benefiting from their visits to me. However, I do welcome this feedback to ensure that I am alert to the effects of my work on people's lives. I have learnt not to assume what outcome possibility is preferable - seeing my role as a fellow traveller along people's journeys rather than being the key to their solutions. This has provided me with an opportunity to practice not being in a hurry to see 'results' or to be set on a certain outcome. (A skill required as a doctor - one that I will always need to practice.)

Recognising the need to consult with the less powerful person in order to be accountable has forced me to address the politics of couples. In the past I can see that I unintentionally worked with a belief that each party is equal in a relationship. If I were to continue to hold a belief that each person in a heterosexual partnership in the 1990s should (and does) have equal say and status, I would miss inequalities of power. If I were to assume that people's interactions in relationships are just part of a process in a family system, if I were to assume that homosexual and heterosexual relationships could be viewed similarly in the therapy room, I would be blind to the inevitable marginalisations that these assumptions would create.

My work as a narrative sexual therapist continues to evolve. What is exciting for me is knowing that inherent in this way of working is the understanding that the ways I work with people in this field today are different from the ways I will be working with them next week or next year. I experience daily the wonders of self-discovery and enrichment as I learn from the knowledges and wisdom of the people I meet in my work. I feel honoured to be a co-author of others' evolving stories of their lives and relationships. Having a commitment to continued self-reflection, I know that my own story - as a therapist, a woman, a partner, and a mother, will continue to evolve over these next weeks and years. I trust that the exploration of new possibilities in my work and my life will continue to bring me joy!

Acknowledgements

Con Tsourtos, for his unquestioning belief in my abilities.

Allan Tudor: my father was a man of unbridled optimism and imagination which enabled him to fulfil his dreams in the face of a longstanding illness. The memory of these qualities has sustained me through many challenges.

Heather Tudor: my mother is a caring woman whose own journey towards self-compassion has been an inspiration to me in my own life and in my work with women.

The following people are those from whom I have learned, and whose acknowledgements have supported me: Cath Kerry, a wonderful feminist teacher who significantly influenced me during my high school years; Greg Smith, Zoy Kazan, Michael White, Leela Anderson, and Vanessa Swan, who have contributed to my growing understanding of narrative.

Jane Tiggeman

Jane Tiggeman is a psychologist and Co-Director of Dulwich Centre, Adelaide. She puts a lot of herself into her work including energy, enthusiasm and passion for people to rise above adversity.

Therapist Through The Looking Glass

'Why are you doing this job anyway?' a father in a high status profession once angrily demanded of me. I had been seeing his 16 year-old-daughter who, like him, was highly intelligent. However, she felt extremely emotionally abused by his treatment of her and the rest of her family. She was very depressed and potentially suicidal. His reason for wanting her to see me was to improve her grades; however, I explained to him that she was on the verge of suicide. He told me he believed in a firm, no-nonsense approach. After I told him that her reason for living was being lost to her and that I believed there were things he could do to make a difference to that, he began to reluctantly listen. However, he kept challenging me throughout the interview, in some ways seeming to scoff at my assessment of his daughter's point of view. It was only when I stood firm and argued passionately with him and when I answered his question about why I do this job, that his attitude changed dramatically, so much so that he shook my hand when he left the session.

When I answered his question, I told him that I had a sense of vocation, that I believed in what I did, that I cared about people, that I had hoped to work alongside people to make a constructive difference in their lives. I said these things and more, but what was important, I believe, was not so much the content of what I said but the life-and-death feelings I conveyed as I spoke. My tone was passionate and full of conviction. I responded strongly with a slight note of anger, partly matching his own.

Putting oneself out there on the line

I've come to realise over time how much passion I have for what I believe therapy means. Therapy involves being prepared to engage with a vast array of presenting problems. The actual core of therapy for me, however, relates to problems involving injustice. I believe that everyone has a right to have the injustice inflicted on them recognised, and some restitution worked out so they can move on and grow in their lives. This involves looking at problems of power and inequity, not only in terms of race, social status, financial opportunity, and gender, but also in terms of the emotional opportunity to have rights to one's feelings, to be able to voice one's core feelings and have these acknowledged, and to show some sense of respect and responsibility towards the feelings of others. In some senses, I see feelings as a great leveller, a way of being able to cut across a lot of other barriers. When one person speaks to another on a feeling level, it makes for greater accountability between them - it allows more understanding and more response. In working with clients, I see my way of formulating questions that help them to access and open up about their beliefs and feelings as a major key to assisting them. I also find that my own emotional/feeling responses to clients constitute one of the most important aspects of my work. It is my view that what I offer in terms of my emotional response is significant to clients, and that they use this to facilitate their processes of change in overcoming their problems.

I am also acutely aware every time I have a therapeutic conversation with a client not only that this conversation hopefully makes a constructive difference to the client but that the conversation and the client's personhood affects me. It is important that, as a therapist, I open myself up to be available to the client. What I offer is genuineness, respect, unconditional positive regard. But within these offerings I also include honesty in being able to tell a client about potential consequences of their behaviour, and I believe in letting them know my value position on certain things. Depending on the relative importance of any difference in the client's position from mine, a conversation might ensue about the safety of responsibility to oneself or others or the community. For example, if a client is having unprotected sex with many different partners, I might raise the question about safety issues for themselves and others. Or if a 30-year-old is having a sexual relationship with a 17-year-old, I would raise the question of responsibility and equity in the relationship. Ultimately it's up to the client to decide unless it is something with the gravity of, for example, a mandatory reporting issue or the threat to endanger the life of another.

I believe opening oneself up to a client is a necessary part of therapy. However, I believe therapists have a choice to do it to a greater or lesser extent depending on their orientation/style/beliefs, and in relation to the particular demands that the interaction with the client presents. The way I open myself up to a client is to look ahead with anticipation and interest, with a willingness to be surprised and influenced by this person I am meeting, often for the first time. I see it as an opportunity to connect with a person at a deeper level (than that which usually occurs in social interaction in the outside world), involving the spirit or essence of the person. Therapy to me is an arena where it is safe for people to 'bare their souls', to be able to discuss their beliefs and the meaning they make of their life experience. This is also something I find personally very fulfilling - that I too have a privilege and responsibility to be able to respond on this level of my spirit in a context of therapeutic relationship to the client. Somehow, for me, this touches on the aspect of having an authentic relationship, one that is totally genuine without any pretence. I believe this is something I have always valued ever since my teenage years, and it is probably why I chose to become a psychologist.

In being open to a client, I frequently experience a sense of excitement at being able to have such a special encounter with a human being. Although I believe it is necessary, opening oneself up to a client can be a perilous activity because we open ourselves up to dealing with emotional pain. Moreover, there are different levels of emotional pain and trauma that you become exposed to. Working with people who have experienced abuse, in particular child sexual abuse, is a prime example of being exposed to deep levels of emotional pain.

Therapist wises up

In the late 1980s I began working with people who had suffered child sexual assault. My first client, Suzanne, a young woman of 18 years, had been continually sexually abused and raped by her male neighbour since she was 11 years old. Her mother had died when she was a child, and her father was a sole parent with five children. Suzanne fell prey to her girlfriend's father. As I worked with her, she taught me a lot - I felt her pain, her feelings of shame, disgust, self-abuse, confusion about her sexuality, helplessness; and I also felt her strength, her voice for justice, her outrage, anger, sadness, and her reclaiming of her sexuality. It was a difficult struggle to help her free herself from the brainwashing and the ongoing rapes. We remained resolute, despite all potential distractions. I felt I made my own changes during this process. As the therapy progressed, the level of complexity of the abuse experience was made clear by Suzanne as she developed greater trust in her connection with me. I became more in touch with a sense of fight inside myself against violation, and I worked with her on getting in touch with her own sense of fight. Suzanne finally gathered the courage to tell me that she was still occasionally being raped by this same perpetrator. It was an amazing victory for both of us when she was able to physically fight off the abuse during one of his assaults. I felt I had experienced an arduous journey, along with her, in facing a sense of helplessness and overcoming this by accessing inner resources to overpower effects of abuse. On one level I felt stronger because of this journey.

Suzanne moved out of home. She began to stand up for her rights and to believe that she was worthy of respect. She decided, some months after we had stopped our sessions, to report the perpetrator and she gave a statement to the police. They visited him and found various torture devices, ropes, etc., and he was charged. I do not know the outcome of the case as we lost contact when she changed jobs.

Suzanne had not told me in graphic detail about the abuse, and I had a sense of its sadistic quality only later when she told me the police had found ropes and instruments of torture. I wonder now if she tried to protect me by minimising the detail. As I have become more experienced in working with survivors of sexual abuse, I have found that clients seem to give only a level of disclosure for which they perceive you and they are ready.

As I reflect on the therapy I did with Suzanne, I realise this was a turning point in my understanding about trust between people in relationships. What I had been taught as a child - to be wary of strangers - took on another significance: that children/adults have to be wary of people who should be trustworthy. I also became aware of a child's vulnerability in being 'tricked' into sexual acts with adult perpetrators.

Anger working for you, rather than against you

Another client, Maryanne, who also experienced child sexual abuse, was the first survivor of child sexual assault I saw in my private practice. She had been sexually abused by her father and brother, from seven years of age, and emotionally abused by her whole immediate family. It was her grandmother and great-grandmother who had nurtured her spirit to keep her alive. Maryanne, prior to entering therapy, had experienced symbols and some types of preliminary hallucinations as she began recalling memories of her childhood abuse. She had incredible determination and righteous anger at the abuse, and we entered into a therapeutic relationship that has lasted over seven years. With the bulk of the work being done in three years, with occasional sessions over subsequent years, she now sees me approximately once every three months. But now she sees my role as assisting her with ongoing life issues, as someone who understands the whole context within which her life has been shaped, and how the past may influence her present concerns.

Working with Maryanne was extremely challenging, particularly as it involved direct verbal threats from her mother towards me. I found it quite frightening to have her mother ring me at home, one day when I was sick, and verbally threaten me about seeing her daughter in therapy. My own mother happened to be visiting me at the time and, while I did not disclose confidential information, I told her of the threat and she responded with a mild degree of outrage and told me that if Maryanne's mother rang again, she would tell her I was not taking calls! My mother's response fortified me, and I am reminded of a realisation I have had for some time: that if it was not for the support of my family and friends, I would not be able to provide clients the quality of therapeutic connection I offer. This work is very demanding and, at times, we as therapists need to have others there for us.

A few years later, Maryanne's mother also threatened Maryanne after she had 'blown the family secret' and confronted her mother and siblings about the abuse that had occurred in the family. Four years of separation followed. Eventually she wrote to her mother and a process of reconciliation, with accountability, was begun. When Maryanne recently separated from her spouse, her mother actively offered her letters of encouragement and support. I would never have seriously considered much hope for wider family reconciliation with acknowledgement of the abuse, but it too is in process.

In our sessions together, Maryanne strongly directed the therapy. Over time I believe she has taken even more voice in giving me helpful guidelines as to what type of conversation she wants from me. Moreover, working with her has been so useful in helping me to see, over a seven year period, how a person's life can be fully reclaimed, and how much healing can occur in the face of very damaging abuse. This has helped me considerably, in my work with other clients, to have a sense of a possible future, of being free from the overwhelming effects of abuse. In Maryanne's situation I have also been able to witness a family that had been split apart by abuse, reconnect years later on a new abuse-free basis.

Maryanne has been a teacher to me in giving me direct feedback (positive and negative) about how she perceives me relating to her in therapy. In my view, she sees me as a person whom she can trust to be honest with her, with whom she can check things out occasionally. She requests my opinion and ideas, and she feels free to disregard them if she so wishes. I myself feel a freedom to offer my ideas, and a freedom to let go of them if they don't seem useful to her. Now we are talking not so much about her story of throwing off remnants of abuse, or reclaiming her life from legacies of it, but more about other problems of life, such as parenting, relationships, etc. Different meanings in her story have emerged now about the types of men she wants in her life, and how their beliefs and actions affect her. It's now more about fine-tuning - the legacies of abuse have been reduced to helpful reminders of anger in the face of injustice, to protect herself and people she loves. Recently, however, she commented that she has realised that sometimes she has too much righteous anger in situations where it may not be appropriate. I was amazed by this comment, as earlier in therapy I had often felt that her anger, at times, seemed disproportionate to the event that triggered it off. At times it felt to me like an assault on my senses.

I never felt it was my place to comment on this anger directly, and it amazed me that it is an aspect of herself she is now advising herself to be aware of. When she first started getting angry with me in our therapy sessions, I found this to be challenging. The force of her anger was something of a shock to me. I found her anger somewhat threatening - this emotional response of mine was very useful in helping me realise I needed to ask the question, 'How much of this anger is to do with the past and not the present?' After we had processed this, the anger that remained directed at me felt appropriate. As is often the case, my emotional response in this situation helped me to get the therapy on track by prompting me to ask the question. She found the question useful and continues to reflect and use it as a tool when considering the appropriateness of her self-righteous anger in different situations.

Reclaiming the little girl inside

The next client I want to speak of is Louise, who came in wanting help with jealousy about her husband, especially when he got close to other women. Louise also told me she had experienced sexual abuse from 5 years of age, by priests and later by her brother. She told me that she felt some of her issues around trust with her husband related to not trusting men due to her abuse. Regardless of the wider context, Louise and I both agreed she needed to assess her husband's loyalty to her. After a few sessions we clarified that some of her concerns about her husband were grounded and she took steps to confront him around this. She then decided she wanted to deal with the excess fear and lack of trust in men - issues that she saw as unhelpful in her life. To do that she decided to deal with her experience of sexual abuse.

She decided the level of detail she wanted to disclose and we began dealing with her spiritual and sexual abuse by priests. I prepared myself to hear her pain by telling myself I had gone through painful stories with Maryanne and others, and I could do it again. However I am aware that, no matter how thorough the preparation, it never diminishes the intensity of the pain; I believe it just makes you a more competent listener. I heard of the full penetration of this little girl at 5 years of age in front of the altar where the priest said, 'Every time you look at the altar you will think of me and it will make you closer to God'. I felt total outrage on her behalf. I expressed some of this to Louise and I contained the rest as I dealt with the fact that the priest had used a type of post-hypnotic suggestion to try to control her and to trick her into believing she should be some sort of sexual servant to God, and to himself as God's representative on earth.

Louise decided to write her story down and I later put it in a full narrative report-form for her as she wanted to take legal action. When I read her notes I would have physical reactions, so I had to be cautious about when to read them. These reactions are difficult to describe but, as a woman, I could almost feel my internal gynaecological organs responding empathically with her experience. Perhaps this was particularly heightened because she had told me she had a malformed uterus because of the abuse, and in later life had several miscarriages prior to having one successful live birth, of her son.

Louise reclaimed her sense of the abused child inside of herself, and we looked at ways that she was re-empowering herself so that she was in control of her relationships, rather than being fearful of them. Louise and her husband became closer as they reclaimed their marriage from the effects of abuse. She has been able to share her story with other survivors, and the Church is currently negotiating compensation (being at the minimum the cost of therapy). Louise's main goal, however, is to have recognition from the Church of her abuse, and she wants it to acknowledge publicly that abuse of children by priests is an abomination and that it will make a commitment to accountability/education of priests in this area.

By January 1992 I thought I had become quite highly skilled in helping people in recovery from child sexual assault, and then I stumbled across the biggest challenge, professionally and personally, of my career. This was organised sadistic abuse, or ritual abuse.

This abuse is the type of abuse which involves pornography of children doing all sorts of oral/vaginal acts, often involving great suffering and pain - sex with animals of all types, torturing and killing animals, use of knives and other objects in all orifices. It also typically involves children being deprived of food, water and sleep, being given drugs, being forced to eat faeces, being locked in cupboards for long periods of time, or in coffins, being made to nearly drown or nearly die but just being spared at the very last moment when they thought they were dead. This abuse involves high levels of organisation - men and women who lead 'double lives'. By day, they are responsible upstanding citizens; by night, sadistic torturers of children. They are people who get sexually aroused by having power over others and by coercing children to perform acts that the children know are wrong. The children end up feeling revulsion at themselves, and the perpetrators tell the children that they are evil and the proof of this lies in the atrocities they have committed. This type of abuse often also has a deliberate goal, to cause dissociation in children to get their mind and body to separate during the torture, much like in an hypnotic state. The perpetrators use brainwashing techniques to implant suggestions into the children's minds, that they can subsequently trigger off to make the children perform acts that the perpetrators require.

Stretching the boundaries

My client Belle came to me originally wanting to work on being able to maintain a long-term relationship with a male. She had recently been through a relationship break-up, and she told me she had been drinking too much, had driven while under the influence of alcohol, and had had some minor car accidents. I asked how she would know when she was over these current problems, and she replied, 'When I felt like a whole person again'. Little did I know at the time that this statement was literal, as she was suffering from fragmentation of her sense of self involving 'dissociative identity disorder', or 'multiple personality disorder'.

Belle then went on to have a series of sessions with me, each time going through a tremendous struggle about whether to return to see me again. She described having nausea reactions prior to seeing me. She disclosed a failed suicide attempt by her father (he had tried to hang himself), when she was 16, that her mother blamed on her. She also revealed that in her early twenties she had seen a church counsellor who, during the therapy, had sex with her, and that she later became aware that he was having sex with other clients. Belle told me that her pre-session nausea was becoming worse and that it was about 'trying to deal with this stuff', and she gradually introduced me to other details of a painful childhood history of torture.

She told me she had experienced dreams the night after seeing me, but that it was like she was 10 years old having a dream. She related that it was about a male workmate of her father's, sexually abusing her, making pornography, and threatening to harm her 6-year-old sister if she did not comply. I began to feel some horror at Belle's unravelling story and now, with this pornography, the story became increasingly full of atrocities which I had difficulty hearing. Elements of Belle being dressed up and then bizarre elements of torture and sexual sadism began emerging. There were also atrocities to dogs and other animals and, of course, to Belle herself. After recounting these events, Belle began having difficulty leaving the sessions; it was hard to help her to calm herself to feel composed enough to leave. I began struggling with what would be of most help to her. I gave her two-hourly sessions, more frequent sessions, and used other techniques for her to try to empower herself. I enlisted the opinions of colleagues, one of whom had a session with Belle and myself. It was this colleague's opinion that Belle had more abuse to disclose, and a few days later the same colleague told me that they thought it might be ritual abuse, something of which I had no understanding at the time.

Soon after, Belle told me about her father sexually violating her from the age of 6: when she was 9 his workmate took over. This began disturbing me more, and I felt angry on her behalf. I ended up telling her that my colleague thought it might be ritual abuse and that we needed to help her establish a wider network of support beyond me. This support network involved friends who would emotionally support her during times she felt in crisis.

Belle soon began to spontaneously enter into regressed altered child states, and she told me awful stories of experiencing sexual/emotional/physical/spiritual damage. Dreadful brainwashing techniques were used upon her. Her level of distress during these sessions were very high and I felt a great need to try and comfort her. I cautiously began, with her permission, to hold her hand and, during the abreactions, to give her hugs in a desperate attempt to comfort the terrified traumatised child who was reliving these horrors as if they were happening all over again. However, this time I was trying to help her to have a different experience, to allow her to give voice to her feelings and her pain, which was not permitted by her torturers. I was allowing her to speak of unspeakable acts, and I was assisting her to free her own narrative from her body and dissociative barriers - to make a nonverbal narrative now a verbal narrative, so that she could give meaning to the trauma and then look at ways of recovering from it, of leaving it in the past and moving forward into the present. The use of touch I also found helpful to assist her to be grounded in the present and to realise at some level that she was still safe in the present as she was, in a sense, 'reviewing' the past. It seemed to be one of the main things that calmed her.

Over time it became clear that she had been abused by large numbers of people in a cult that appeared to be satanic, and that she saw herself as unclean, defiled and evil. The perpetrators had seemingly trained her as a type of sexual slave, and she had experienced many near-death incidents. They had forced her to commit atrocities on other children, animals and adults, and had convinced parts inside herself that she was evil and belonged to that cult.

During this early 6-month phase in the work with Belle, I went through huge changes in myself. Initially I thought I must be working with something that was very rare and that I was probably the only therapist in Australia dealing with such a sinister problem. I was unsure of who I could confide in, apart from my partner and colleague, Gregory Smith, who provided me with invaluable support.

The horrors I had been privy to, I knew, were sadistic and criminal, and I began to become concerned about my safety and Belle's. At one stage I suggested to her that I anonymously report it to the Police as sexual assault. I even asked her permission to ring Legal Aid anonymously in order to see what the legal position was for a child who had been coerced to torture and kill. The Legal Aid adviser was quite sympathetic and said if it was against my client's will she would not be legally responsible, particularly given she was also a minor at the time.

Our therapy sessions continued. I finally found a copy of *Nursery Crimes* by Dr Anne Schlebaum, a psychiatrist in Sydney. What Anne described in her paper seemed to be what Belle had been subjected to. I eagerly wrote to Anne and she forwarded me some references. I also tried to talk with colleagues about this sadistic abuse but few people had heard of it.

By now I was having a very difficult time working with Belle. She was at times so distressed that I was seeing her excessively, and she was ringing me regularly at home. She became suicidal, and I felt she needed psychiatric assessment. One Saturday I finally got her to agree to this, and I accompanied her to Casualty at a local hospital. Some hours later, after quite an ordeal, she was admitted. After this hospital stay we managed to arrange for a psychiatrist to see her on an ongoing basis. The psychiatrist was very supportive and we divided the workload between us; the psychiatrist saw Belle twice a week focussing on here-and-now issues, while I dealt with issues of addressing the trauma from the past and reclaiming herself in the present.

Belle and I attended a conference in Adelaide for survivors of ritual abuse. That conference was run by survivors of ritual abuse who experienced 'multiple personality' and 'dissociation'. Many moving accounts of survival were shared at this workshop, which was a lifeline for me as I met other colleagues working in this area with whom I could network. In particular I met Anne-Marie Hayes, a social worker at Adelaide Women's Community Health Centre. Anne-Marie and I went on to have regular meetings to provide support for ourselves and to discuss treatment ideas, and we have become good friends and colleagues.

At the workshop, the condition 'multiple personality disorder' (MPD) was mentioned. I had not seen any evidence of this condition with Belle so I convinced myself that she was a survivor of ritual abuse and that she did not have MPD, or 'dissociative identity disorder' as it is now named. However, it was only a matter of weeks until Belle told me that she heard voices inside her head and she thought she had a fragmented sense of self with different parts of herself clamouring to be heard. I began to feel overwhelmed, wondering if I was skilled enough to deal with her problem.

A few months after I begain working with Belle, I started seeing Faye, a client who was going through divorce. She told me she had been raped by a medical person while she was an inpatient in a hospital. On one occasion during a session when her angry ex-husband attacked her verbally, Faye just seemed to go into her own world and detach from reality. I asked the ex-husband to leave and I tried to help her. I told her I felt she would need to go to hospital for assessment as she seemed in an altered state and I did not know how to help her.

As Faye's history unravelled, it became clear she was dependent on heroin, had a history of child sexual abuse by an uncle, and had had several hospital admissions over the years. She was also very intelligent and held down a good job. Over time I came to understand that she would go into dissociated states when under certain types of stress. As I reviewed her notes one day I realised she had begun to talk to me about symbols and some ritualistic elements of her abuse. I encouraged Faye to be open with me, assuring her that whatever the truth, however small or big it was, I would support her. Some weeks later she began having flashbacks about sadistic elements of her abuse, and over time she began to disclose similar stories to Belle's: of torture perpetrated on her, and ways she was forced to torture others. I thus found myself with another client who had experienced horrendous organised abuse by groups of people.

I decided, with Belle's and Faye's permission, to introduce them to each other to provide another source of support for them. I also wondered if we could look at ways we could work as a team. Overall this worked well, although at times some child parts of the clients occasionally competed with each other for my attention. However, the gains were that they could support each other generally and in their individual relationship with me.

Entering metamorphosis with the client: from caterpillar to butterfly

I have now been working with Belle and Faye for approximately four years. The work has been extremely difficult but not without its rewards. We have developed a close rapport and an understanding of the importance of this therapy in helping each of them to reclaim themselves from the effects of the atrocities of men's and women's inhumanity to humanity. We have laughed, cried, shared our fears and hopes together. I have chosen to bear witness to the horrible atrocities they experienced, and this has been at once both a privilege and a trial. Working with these women has both strengthened and weakened me. I have grown stronger in realising I can cope with and face incredible pain and suffering and find a way to help, but I have grown weaker in giving out my energy in a bid to try to keep them afloat. Many times they have seemingly been close to death or further torture, drug overdoses, self-mutilation, or re-abuse by other cult members. I have had to endure isolation and ridicule from some members of the professional community during my attempts to help these women. In my personal life it has taken a toll. These atrocities have a way of stalking you - in your unconscious, through intense fear for yourself and those you love. I noted at times I would be hypervigilant and easily startled and anxious, occasionally having feelings of possible threats from perpetrators. I also had trouble sleeping at night, which was further aggravated at times by Belle ringing me in a suicidal state in the early hours of the morning. I also had regular out-of-hours calls from Faye when she was in crisis, feeling terror, or when she found herself in dissociated states, ringing me from public phone boxes not knowing where she was or how she got there. I found that my family and friends were generally very supportive, but over time they also began having difficulty at times understanding the severity of the trauma with which I was working.

I remember having a dream early in my work with Belle in which I felt I was trying to save her, but that she, in her distress, was pulling me under the water, inadvertently drowning me. I talked to her about this dream as I saw it as a sign I needed to have more boundaries in my work. Every time I put more boundaries in place she got upset and felt I was rejecting her. This made me feel guilty but I knew I did not have a choice. So I put more boundaries in place. She would constantly 'test' me to see if I was trustworthy, as she had never been able to trust adults before, so why me now? Later in my work with her, I had a dream involving intense fear in which I was in a cafe with my partner. He had gone to order a coffee at the bar, and a woman at the adjacent table asked who I was. I said, 'a therapist from Adelaide'. She introduced herself as a member of a sadistic cult. I remember shooting into the air with my hair standing on end! I knew this dream represented the intense fear I had experienced and was trying to handle. I shared my feelings with my partner, Greg; with Anne-Marie Hayes; and with other friends at times, and these people have kept me going.

During my work with survivors of child sexual assault and torture, I have become more aware of certain qualities in myself, and I have also learnt from clients about areas in my work that I would benefit from developing further. Qualities I have become aware of include my perseverance to keep working at difficult problems in the face of extreme conditions; patience to keep working slowly and steadily, building on small changes; determination to stick by what I believe in; honesty and courage to say how I feel; my capacity to care and show empathy, and love and anger, and at times a sense of rage in the face of sadistic injustice, and my capacity to channel this energy in constructive ways.

I have learned the hard way that boundaries need to be firm and clear and constantly put in place and highlighted. I have learned about my capacity for giving, and at times I have given when my own personal resources seemed almost empty, like a reservoir that was being steadily drained. I have also learned about the importance of filling myself up and pacing myself in terms of what I give out.

My work with sexual abuse, and ritual abuse in particular, has made a significant impact on my life in terms of my belief system, including my view of humanity. People are incredibly complex beings and are motivated for a variety of different reasons. I have tried to understand abuse from numerous viewpoints. Why does it happen? Research quoted by Judith Herman in her recent seminar in Sydney indicated that a considerable percentage of abuse involves repeating a learnt pattern, however, there is also a percentage of abusers who do it purely for the opportunity to have complete power and control over others. Fortunately this latter group are in the minority. It is clear that some people do take sadistic pleasure in the suffering of others. This is abhorrent to me and I find it extremely difficult to come to terms with. Have these people never suffered themselves? Or are they so determined never to suffer that they make everyone else suffer, making others submit to them out of their own fear?

In some of the sadistic cults I understand there is a belief that actively inflicting torture on children makes them strong and so the children who survive are better able to cope with life. However, it is also clear to me that people who perform sadistic practices in cults use conditioning techniques to associate pain and pleasure. This would appear to be a way of exploiting control over primary drives such as sex and aggression. And, of course, using pain and deprivation can cause victims to become dissociated, so they can be even further abused. Basically I have realised that these torturers use psychological techniques involving brainwashing procedures in order to be extremely destructive and to gratify their own selfish needs for power, lust, or whatever. In my mind there is no morally acceptable justification for it whatsoever. However, I have also had to confront the fact that these dualities of good versus evil are not so clear. Many studies have indicated that any person placed in conditions of extreme deprivation and pain is capable of becoming a torturer of others in order to save themselves. I used to think if I was put in a hostile situation and I had a choice of torturing or being tortured, I would be able to resist, and I might be able to for a time. However, I now realise that I, like anyone else, would probably succumb given the right damaging conditions, especially if the option to take my own life was also taken away.

The core question returns for me. What does a person want in their life? Do they want to die remembering themselves as helping others, in contributing towards everyone having something out of life, or do they want to just satisfy their own desires at the expense of others? Of course, some people want something in between. Concepts of good and evil are reassuring but, I believe, are probably not so useful. Perhaps it is more useful to think of one's capacity to indulge in both sets of acts, and of our opportunity to choose which overall path we wish to follow. Of course, accountability to others for our behaviours is essential, and I see striving for compassion towards others and self as being a useful guiding principle.

My views on people have changed. My sense of trust in others is more finely tuned. I do not take for granted that people can be trusted. However, I also do not assume they cannot. In practice I think this means I tune into others more carefully, especially around care-taking of children or vulnerable others. I also talk openly with people who are willing to listen about the fact that torturing of children does exist, that these people are sadistic. Without becoming hysterical, we need to be aware of this to protect children against these potential perils. I strongly feel that, as therapists, we need to confront community denial that sadistic acts against our children go on. I believe each person needs to ask themselves the political question, 'Do I want to protect children from violence and abuse even if it means having to confront some painful realities for myself?' I was a child once - what would I have wanted the adult's answer to have been?

During the countless hours of reading I have done around this type of abuse, I have realised that Freud discovered the existence of, and spoke of, the effects of child sexual abuse in 1896 in his theory of seduction. Unfortunately, at this time he experienced such opposition and lack of acceptance of the existence of such abuse, he retracted his theory. Masson in his book 'Assault on Truth' describes how Freud wrote to Fleiss after he had given a paper on 'The Theory of Seduction', exclaiming how isolated and professionally ostracised he felt because colleagues would not accept his theory. When I read this I could relate to my own experience of working with ritual abuse and dealing with a high level of societal and, at times, professional denial of the problem. Judith Herman in her book 'Trauma and Recovery' describes how it is her belief that issues included in coming to terms with trauma, such as child sexual abuse, can only emerge in a 'window of opportunity' when the current political climate is able to allow them to be voiced, rather than be rendered invisible by the culture, and dealt with by societal denial.

A number of clients, including survivors of abuse, tell me from time to time how my contribution to therapy has made a significant difference to their life. This is what gives me hope and enthusiasm to continue with my work, to see my work as meaningful and worthwhile. I find it very spiritually uplifting to see a person free themselves from the effects of abuse.

Working with organised sadistic abuse is not for the faint-hearted, but it is tremendously rewarding to see adult survivors begin to lead a life where they are no longer under the control of torturers of children. I also feel that Belle and Faye will go on (like other survivors) to work to prevent this type of abuse happening to children in the future. I have tremendous admiration for them both, and I feel privileged to have shared some of my life with theirs.

It has become more possible for survivors of the trauma of child sexual assault to speak out and free themselves from the 'unspeakable' story. However, while more 'ordinary' stories of child sexual assault are able to be faced by society, there is still an extensive struggle and denial about the more extreme sadistic abuses to children. I believe it is a challenge to therapists to be able to have courage to hear each survivor's story, to help each develop a verbal narrative so they can free themselves from the negative effects of such admirable survival techniques as dissociation. However, as therapists, we must also look after ourselves in the process so that we are not taking on their pain. Instead we need to find helpful boundaries, containment processes and colleagues with whom to consult. In this way we can allow the toxic secrecy of men's and women's inhumanity to humanity to be acknowledged, thereby making a significant step towards overcoming it - in the process, two people emerge from the swim and no-one drowns along the way.

References

Ferenzi, S. 1933:
'Confusion of tongue between adults and the child.' In *Final Contributions to the Problems and Methods of Psychoanalysis, pp.155-167.* (1985) New York: Basic Books.
Gibson, J.T. & Haritos-Satouros, M. 1986:
'The education of a torturer.' *Psychology Today,* November.
Herman, J. 1992:
Trauma and Recovery. Pandora Basic Books.
Masson, J. 1993:
Against Therapy. London: Harper Collins.
Schlebaum, A. 1990:
'Nursery crimes - A perfect little holocaust in the suburbs.' *The Patient and the Law and the Professional.* Proceedings of the 11th Annual Congress of Australian & New Zealand Association of Psychiatry, Psychology & Law. Melbourne.

Acknowledgements

I would like to thank the following people as having a central role in inspiring and supporting me in the work that I do. Because of them, I have been able to offer to my work energy, enthusiasm, and passion for people to rise above adversity. I sincerely thank them for being there for me during trying times in my work.

My grandmother Edith May Russ, now 88 years of age, has been a strong influence on my life in helping me to have a sense of delight in others and a belief that most problems can be overcome, and that 'life is too short' to be caught up in problems. My grandmother's sense of belief in me has inspired me to be able to offer this in my work to others.

Gregory Smith, my partner, has shown unrelenting belief in my specialness and this helps me to reaffirm ongoing belief in myself and the value of my work.

My parents, Shirley and John, and my sister Louise, and brother Mark, plus their partners Les and Enrica, have shown loving support and patience during the hard therapeutic times. Maddison, my 8-year-old niece, is a very special person to me, and her talents and empathy to others are a special gift that my grandmother has also had a special role in handing on. Jordan, my 5-year-old nephew, is the best little boy I know who offers mischievousness and energy - a welcome distraction from the potential seriousness of the problems of life.

Fiona is a clear thinking person who keeps me grounded and in touch with what is important in life. I feel indebted to her in many ways.

Clare is another loyal, special friend who recognises my talents and abilities, and who inspires me to fight on for the rights of others and myself.

Anne-Marie has shown me what patience is, and her collegial support has sustained my work. She has been a soul workmate to me, and is now also a good friend.

Marta is a positive force, a colleague who never hesitates to offer whatever she can to help.

Heather has accepted me (warts and all), and our relationship has developed over the years.

Jan has offered ongoing friendship and collegial support, and reminded me (some time ago) that anything worth wanting is worth fighting for.

Dave has been a special male friend who has shown acceptance and understanding of me in the difficult nature of my work with abuse.

Celia (in some ways an ethereal spirit) inspires me to break free and develop the creative side of myself.

Aerobics classes have also played an important part in helping me to deal with frustration of anger from working with effects of abuse. My aerobics instructors (and friends), Mike and Chris, have been an inspirational force to keep smiling despite any pain (in or out of aerobics classes), and have reminded me that 'when the going gets tough the tough get going'!

Judith has been a healing force for my mind, body and spirit.

My cats Ditto, Chops and Tinkerbell are therapeutic cats who are also committed to helping others, including me, when their busy schedule permits.

David Denborough

When David's inside and not sitting in front of his computer, or on the phone, he tries to be near pianos. Outside, the walk along the cliffs between Bronte and Bondi always seems to reach out to him and, now that he's all fitted out with his newly acquired prescription goggles(!), he'll actually be able to see what's in the Bondi water. Whether that makes him swim more or less I guess we'll soon see. He'd love people to write to him c/- Dulwich Centre, Adelaide.

Becoming Squarehead, Becoming Gubba

For the last two and half years I have made the journey from my white middle-class home in inner city Sydney to work within a men's maximum security prison. It has felt at times as if each working day I migrate from one world to another and back. This article seeks to explore how such an experience has invited me to consider what it means to be a white middle-class Australian, and how such explorations have enriched my life.

Introduction: Crossing boundaries

When I first stepped up to the metallic gates of the prison in which I work I was overwhelmed by the structure itself. Rarely, if ever, have I felt so small, so insignificant. There was also such a strong sense of history, as if the sandstone walls were harbouring such secrets. I know now that various Koori inmates and workers experience the spirits of various parts of the prisons. Where possible, those who are housed in what were once the cells of the condemned burn oils to free the souls.

The wind is always howling across the bay on which the prison is built. Before I move from one world to the next I take a slightly deeper breath than usual and try to hold the colours of the outside world in my mind. Having stepped up to the wall, I ring the buzzer and, after the obligatory wait, the grey solid steel gate in front of me opens. I grunt a 'G'day' as I ruffle through my wallet until I find my ID. Having flashed it coolly and received a nod of recognition for my efforts, I walk on through.

I notice that my posture has changed. My shoulders are back slightly further than usual, there's a tightness across my neck, and I've hidden every sign of effeminacy from my walk. It's the same posture I held on the football field all those years ago. Even my voice is different, lower somehow, more laid back, and my language full of 'mate' and a litany of adjectives that I've only come to use since working inside.

Unfortunately the work shifts move the prison officers around so much that I rarely know the officer on the gate by name. It would make a significant difference if I did and I tell myself that I must make a greater effort.

While waiting, always waiting, for the next set of gates to be opened, the same stale air greets my face. On my tongue it feels like it's been through everyone's cigaretted lungs before it has got to me. Finally the gate swings open, I walk through, and it closes behind me. I am back inside.

I stride through the centre of the prison, the 'circle', and there, as always, I find sweet relief. For every story of sorrow in prison there is a story of triumph of spirit. Meticulously painted on the front of each cell block are huge murals. No place is uglier than prison, no art more beautiful than these murals. Amongst the grey and the desolate, in the least expected of places there is always beauty, resistance and life.

Becoming squarehead

> *Inherited privilege, and the assumption of it, is something one carries in one's very bones.* (Penelope 1994, p.54)

Working in prisons has meant coming in contact with communities that are not my own. To find myself teaching a welfare/sociology class to long-termers in a maximum security prison was to find myself transported into a culture very different from the white middle-class world to which I am accustomed. One morning I naively asked the group what they would have called me had we met as children. Without a moment's hesitation and with a dead-pan expression, one guy replied, 'a squarehead'. Unfazed, I asked what this meant, and with a large grin he explained, 'a stuck-up poof who can't fuck'. My lessons had begun.

At this stage, in hysterics and with laughter filling the room, I managed to articulate that I would have thought of them as 'westies' (from the western suburbs), but that I wouldn't have dared call them this to their faces, as I would have been terrified of being beaten up by the violent, ugly and stupid young men that I believed they were!

Believe it or not, in hindsight this was the beginning of ongoing attempts to build partnerships across a class divide. Their naming of my middle-class experience challenged me to explore and articulate what it means to be middle-class. It was the beginning of an ongoing process of rewriting and understanding my life through the experiences of working-class people. It is this process that I refer to as 'becoming squarehead'.

What does it mean to be middle-class?

One of the first things that was absolutely clear was that they were much more familiar with the term 'westie' than I was with the term 'squarehead'. To be middle-class means that one's culture is rarely the 'object' of analysis. We 'professionals' too often maintain our invisible privilege or our privilege of invisibility. In this way we avoid acknowledging how we have benefited from class relations and, instead, blame those who are disadvantaged by such relations for resisting. Everyday in prisons professionals such as myself deny the impact of class relations by mystifying the process of imprisonment, by calling prisons 'correctional centres', by claiming that self-harm is 'manipulative', by diagnosing those who challenge professional practices as 'difficult' and unworthy of 'help', and by understanding crimes as caused by individual pathology.

For me, being a middle-class professional meant I assumed that I could develop a curriculum and deliver it in my language. Somehow my university degree was supposed to give me the credentials to judge and assess others and their work. These were the skills for which I was employed, the reason why I was to be paid. It is a part of middle-class experience to assume that such 'professional' skills are valuable to those with whom we work. Often we 'professionals' can participate in such practices of power and domination, all the while keeping our assumptions, privilege and cultural motivations hidden.

By naming me as 'squarehead', however, such privilege was challenged. I was no longer 'normal' in a middle-class world, I was a 'squarehead' in a 'westies' world. It was me who used a different language, wore different clothes, held different values. I've never done time, I have no tattoos, don't know how to read a form guide, don't smoke, indeed I'm asthmatic. I don't do weights, and I don't even play a sport any more. When different guys constantly asked me how I had made the corners on my wooden briefcase, I had to respond that my last woodworking attempt was in year nine when I inadvertently created a triangular car.

A squarehead reflects

By naming me as squarehead, the men with whom I work were inviting me to acknowledge the ways in which I have benefited from class relations, and to realise that they have often been on the other end of such dynamics. They were demanding of me that I resist the common middle-class assumption that people in prison are in some way more racist, dominating, and/or sexist, than those not in prison. There is no doubt that prisons breed violence, racism, and sexism, but when people enter them they are likely to be doing so because they have less money and/or darker skin than others, rather than because of some deficiency or oppressive characteristic. The most invigorating, open and honest discussions I have ever had with men about gender and sexual violence have occurred in prisons, while the most difficult, frustrating and crazy-making conversations have occurred with middle-class men such as myself who profess to be 'pro-feminist'.

Becoming squarehead has similarly altered my views on crime. Where once my view of crime involved stereotypical views of working-class men committing property offences or street crimes, now the first thing that flashes into my mind is the crime that is prison. I think of the crime that we middle-class Australians commit by allowing those who live in poverty to be criminalised and brutalised. I realise now that the use of prisons does not reduce violence but instead both creates it and moves it around so that it occurs behind prison walls, between working-class people. It was a further shock to my squarehead consciousness to discover that many people who commit armed robberies understand their actions through sophisticated analyses of capitalism, and that some are knowledgeable of whole histories of which I am completely unaware, histories of worker and prison movements.

Perhaps more profound, however, has been recognising the specific practices or emphases of my middle-class culture, how they differ from working-class cultures, and the effects of such differences. The very conversation that began my process of becoming squarehead would never have occurred in the adult middle-class culture from which I come. The directness, honesty, and the burly sense of humour that were essential to challenge my middle-class experience are important aspects of working-class cultures. The emphasis on politeness and reserve that characterises my middle-class culture profoundly supports the maintenance of the status quo. Whenever a member of an oppressed group expresses their outrage, their claims can be disregarded simply because they are not expressed in middle-class 'adult' ways.

Christian McEwen describes middle-class 'niceness' as camouflage:

Upper class betterness is built on centuries of other people's work. It is built on land and industry maintained by other people, income and profits got at their expense. Most of those involved are well aware of this, and the feelings (understandably) are strong. Guilt and fear and ignorance on the part of those in power, anger and resentment on the part of the workers, threaten to burst forth at any minute. Under the circumstances, niceness is a very useful tool. It gives the upper classes some sort of camouflage to operate behind, at the same time as it aims to distract everyone from what is actually going on. (1994, p.271)

Such challenges have meant coming to terms with the fact that the entire view of professionalism in which I had been enculturated is at best irrelevant, and at worst offensive, to those with whom I work. It has meant recognising that teaching is a two-way process - except initially when the only person learning was me! It has meant recognising that the only ways in which I can be effective within a culture that is not my own is to build relations of trust.

At the initiative of those with whom I work, we have created spaces in which men can share their stories and strategies of survival, build on positive understandings, and create new ways of relating to, and supporting, one another. Within such groups my role as an 'outsider' is to ask questions, as do other group members, and to share my life experiences, as do other group members. Obviously sometimes the questions that I ask and the things I share are from different perspectives than those of others. Sometimes an outsider can honour stories of resistance to injustice, or notice contradictions in ways that those inside a total institution cannot. Similarly, I have access to information and resources that those with whom I work obviously don't. We try to create what bell hooks describes as access to *forms of education for critical consciousness, that are essential to the decolonisation process* (1994, p.5). We explore how we have resisted injustice, how we have participated in injustice, and how we can support each other to further resist in constructive ways. We link daily prison struggles to a broader politics - politics of gender, race and class. And all the while we are developing new skills to use to survive and challenge injustice. When possible we produce something tangible from such groups, be it a recorded song, a video to send to schools, a book honouring the stories of survival, or transcribed interviews to educate others. These become resources for further groups, further change.

Such a process is far slower than traditional 'teaching'. When the guys with whom I have built trusting relationships are moved to other prisons it takes time to build new relationships. Prison is superb at encouraging self-doubt, not only for those incarcerated, but also in workers. Self-doubt paralyses and maintains the status quo. Nonetheless there are ripples from such work, and it is important for me to recognise them.

Retracing histories

Becoming squarehead has not only revealed to me oppressive 'professional' practices, but has also opened up new ways of understanding aspects of my life. Incidents I once viewed as 'normal' I now see as products of privilege. Middle-class privilege meant that the values being espoused at my school were not in conflict with those of my family. It meant never hearing conversations about money for the entirety of my childhood. One of the reasons I can write this article is because middle-class privilege has allowed me to be comfortable with the written word, with academia. Being middle-class let me see police as people who would protect me rather than assault me. It meant that my family was never intruded upon by the state, and that therefore the only institution I had to deal with as a child was school.

Perhaps, most importantly, middle-class privilege has meant having the opportunity to become rich and powerful. So saturated with opportunities was my childhood that when I received a high school matriculation mark that enabled me to study medicine or law, this represented to me not an opportunity but more of the same competitive scramble.

At the same time, becoming squarehead has revealed to me the influences of a working-class history on one side of my family that has been hidden and silenced. The pressure to appear middle-class and the benefits for doing so must have outweighed, for my grandparents, the value of maintaining their connection to working-class culture. How impossibly difficult it must be to move from a westie world into a world of squareheads! Whether my family notices it or not, our working-class history lives on in the generosity of my cousins who, even in times of great hardship, prioritise the giving of gifts. It lives on through my father and his familiar cry of 'life is too short', the ways in which he lives day by day, and his attitude to money. I see now that my mother's request to 'keep your options open' is born out of a different, middle-class tradition. I see how her astute planning and distribution of family resources derives in some ways from generations of having the option and privilege to save and accumulate. I see how my respect and passion for education, books and knowledge, have been nurtured by a middle-class culture. I feel that my life has been greatly enriched by both traditions.

I wonder if the challenges of those with whom I work influence me in the ways that they do because they resonate with my (hidden) family histories. I recognised only while writing this paper that on one side of my family a great-great-grandfather was a working-class man who spent time imprisoned, while another was the first Chief Justice of Australia who imprisoned others.

No matter the mixed heritage, it is clear to me, and to those with whom I work, that I am a squarehead. Becoming aware of this has changed the person that I am. It has opened new landscapes for me to explore, new histories and new futures. The men who originally challenged me have moved on now, transported to other prisons, but their laughter and words remain with me.

Becoming Gubba

Across the country there are many different Indigenous Australian words to describe non-Indigenous people, including gubs, gubbas, murantawi, balanda and gadiya (Egan 1994, p.77). As I am from NSW and my interactions have largely been with Koori people who know me as a gubba, that is the term which I have adopted to explore my experience as a non-Indigenous Australian.

It is a reflection on race relations in this culture that it wasn't until I worked behind bars that I had any meaningful contact with Indigenous Australian culture or people. Todd Gordon was the first person to tell me that I was, in his language, a gubba - a white person. More recently I became aware that the word gubba is derived from the word 'government'. It seems a particularly useful word to locate our history as white Australians in relation to the state, to the police, to prisons, and to the invasion of this country. Seeing myself through a different language was once again the beginning of a process of rewriting and understanding my life, this time through the experiences of Indigenous Australians. It is this process that I refer to as 'becoming gubba'.

The events of one afternoon further shifted the ground under my feet. I had been invited by a number of Koori men, with whom I had been working, to sit in on a planning meeting for an upcoming Koori project. I was the only gubba present and also the only prison employee. As the conversation took a particular tack, I began to express my concerns about particular decisions that looked as if they were soon to be made. After further discussion, a number of men in the group began to get very agitated with me, until finally it was suggested in no uncertain terms that I leave the room.

As I walked out I realised that I had violated the sacredness of the invitation that I had received. I had spoken in a space in which I had no right to speak. It was the first time that I realised that there were places and times in which my skin colour, my ancestry, my privilege, meant that it was oppressive for me to speak. As a white person I had believed this land was mine to travel and speak in wherever I chose. Becoming gubba has meant, and continues to mean, recognising that I have responsibilities concerning how, when and where I travel, speak and act. That afternoon also taught me a further important lesson. Having recognised the ways in which I had inadvertently replicated white supremacy, I wrote a letter to the group and dialogue was maintained. The generosity of the Indigenous Australian men involved made it clear to me that being yelled at was an invitation to challenge the ways I was relating, not a demand for our relationships to end.

What does it mean to be white?

Exploring what it means to be gubba is only one aspect of many necessary for me to truly examine what it means to be white and to challenge racism. The following pages do not in any detail attempt to struggle with how I, as a white Australian, participate in racist practices towards other immigrants to this country. Obviously such issues are of great importance. Problematising what it means to be gubba is a starting point for me to explorations of race and racism.

Being white has meant that I haven't had to think or feel about issues of racism until well into my twenties. I have had the privilege of not noticing my own skin colour. White privilege has meant that I have been able to live in a land conquered by my ancestors and ignore the implications.

It has meant that I can go shopping without feeling as if everyone is looking at me in case I may shop-lift. White supremacy has meant that I have been able to take for granted that I belong here simply because I belong nowhere else. It has meant not noticing the irony that white racism has caused those whose home this country has been for tens of thousands of years, to often feel excluded and unwelcome.

Fundamentally, to be white in Australia has meant denying that I am a gubba. It has meant denying that there is any process I need to go through, any work I need to do in relation to the place that I find myself, the actions of my ancestors, and the racism that continues today. Being white has meant being able to claim that we can look only at the present and the future, that to take history seriously is to 'look backwards' and brings only 'guilt'.

It seems to me that the Indigenous Australian men with whom I was working were challenging such views. They were challenging me to see myself not as simply 'normal', or as generically 'Australian', but specifically as gubba. They were challenging my comfortableness, my privilege, and at the same time inviting me to develop a greater understanding of my place here.

For me, listening to Indigenous Australians' stories of this country's history, the stories that have been for so long silenced, is a first step. I have to consciously allow myself to be affected by these stories, to stop myself from disconnecting from them. I have had to recognise that those who did the killing were doing so on behalf of people like me. They believed that their actions were connected to us, even if we try to disconnect ourselves from them. As Duncan Graham writes:

> We are the recipients of stolen goods. The men who cleared the land of trees and rocks to grow crops and graze stock also cleared the land of its owners and users. Those invaders said they demolished and destroyed and killed for the sake of future generations. We are all part of that future planned by others. Like you, my family and I find shelter, warmth, profit, security, pleasure, comfort and joy from living on the proceeds of thieves and killers. (1994, p.107)

Becoming gubba for me does not mean viewing shame as an end to be avoided, but rather a part, along with exhilaration, sadness and joy, of coming to terms with the histories of this country and its ongoing racism, honouring the experiences of Indigenous Australians, and finding ways to move forwards. For me the connection to history comes also through my direct family relations. My great-great-grandfather sent many Indigenous Australians to their deaths as a judge, and ignored their rights wholeheartedly in the constitution which he played a part in constructing. I was never aware of these connections until very recently. One generally has to search to hear of how one's family has contributed to the genocide of Indigenous Australians.

Of course, such contributions to genocide are not over, they are continuing. Becoming gubba not only involves a new relationship to the histories of this country, but also recognising the legacies of such histories and the ways we perpetuate them. For instance, when I began work in the prison system I was most frightened of the darkest skinned men and as such was less likely to offer them my services or hear their stories.

Similarly, the group I work for, Men Against Sexual Assault (Sydney), has perpetuated the silence that surrounds histories of sexual assault in this country. We have ignored that the men who we read about in history books, the pioneers, explorers, politicians, statesmen, were also the men who raped indigenous women and forced the offspring of such assaults to live on reserves. We have ignored the history of sexual assault on missions, in homesteads, and in boys' homes.

As Victor Lewis states in the film *The Color of Fear* (1991), the most toxic, lethal racism is perpetrated by 'very nice folks' who would claim they are against injustice. Such a realisation rings true in my life as I am confronted with the ways I am blind to racist beliefs and practices.

Even the ways in which I think are within white supremacist frameworks. The highly mechanistic metaphors which we use in white-Anglo culture to understand ourselves and our relationships have only become obvious to me in their comparison with the metaphors of Koori culture. I recall listening to Vicky Barrett when she was to present to white teachers on issues of Indigenous Australian culture. She described a feeling of pain in her stomach, which she understood as a metaphor of pregnancy. She hoped the session was to give birth to new ways of understanding. The contrast of Indigenous Australian ways of speaking to the world of academia, in which one tries to assert one's 'objective facts' over others, is apparent. Being invited into these other ways of viewing life has been a thoroughly enriching experience. At the same time it has shown me glimpses of the myriad of ways in which race and culture are a part of the very air we breathe, and how challenging white supremacy involves noticing what we gubbas seldom notice.

Retracing histories

Becoming gubba is also involving retracing entire histories of my life and seeing them through different lenses. Some of my earliest memories involve playfully exploring the mountain behind our suburban Canberra house. I guess it was a hill really, cleared for grazing. I suppose now that once this land was occupied by the Ngarigo people but, by the time my small feet were traipsing (trespassing) amongst the rocks and dried grass, there was no sign of their earlier explorations - or at least to my untrained five-year-old eyes. My relationship to these memories is now changed as part of the process of becoming gubba. It is hard to describe how, but my sense of place is altered by knowing that other people's feet had explored 'my mountain' for thousands of years. To discover that the Black Mountain where we used to picnic was once Blacks' Mountain, or that the turrets on country houses were built for the express purpose of shooting Indigenous Australians, alters my entire perception of myself and my country.

Never when at school did I have to think of myself as white, only that others were 'not white'. Constantly I would define others, with the support of white supremacist culture, in relation to my colour, my place, my culture. Looking back I realise now that the boys who were called 'boong' must have been Indigenous Australians. At the time, so whitewashed was our school and my background that I didn't even make the connection. Another boy in my year was referred to as 'nip'; another constantly taunted rather than praised for his soccer skills and Greek background; and 'Jew' was a generic insult.

I did nothing to either enquire as to the origin of such nicknames, or try to stop such racial division or slurs. From the make-up of the student and teacher populations, to the language used and history taught, my school was a white school. And me? I was simply Australian and normal - the subject of no taunts. The language we spoke was mine, the sports we played the same that my father played.

Even my understandings of my teenage years are altered by hearing the stories of Indigenous Australians. The nihilism and emptiness of my adolescence that I have analysed through theories of gender and youth powerlessness, I now also understand as a product of white ways. The individualism and competitiveness that I have often called 'capitalism' or 'dominant masculinity' perhaps I should call white people's ways.

Cultural histories

Understanding what it means to be white obviously involves tracing the histories of one's ancestors, for there one can find meanings upon which to build. My Anglicised name was invented just prior to the Second World War, changed from van den Bergh, a Dutch name, in order that our family not be confused with the Afrikaaners in South

Africa who were supporting Hitler. My grandfather, who had Flemish and Dutch ancestry, later became a British Israelite, believing that the British were the lost tenth tribe of Israel. Somewhere along the line, mainly due to British imperialism, we lost all connection to our Dutch heritage. My white privilege and my middle-class status converge in this story, in that my grandfather and grandmother, both from working-class families, moved from England to become privileged whites in the newly conquered Rhodesia (now Zimbabwe). The change of status probably enabled my father to meet my wealthy Australian mother years later in England. My very existence is therefore tied up in the colonisation of Africa.

When I trace the histories of Anglo culture, it is clear that its dominant stories dictate a competitive, individualistic way of seeing the world, a spirituality of a hierarchical, judgemental God, and a concept of community based around 'the family' and the rule of the father. My blood-lines encourage conquering, using (or now saving) the environment, rather than seeing ourselves and the earth as an intricate relationship.

But to be white fortunately is not to be monolithic. Even within cultures of imperialist history there are a multitude of myths, meanings and traditions on which to build. I am excited at the prospect of searching my ancestries for alternative cultural meanings on which I will be proud to build. I can acknowledge that even within my great-great-grandfather Samuel Griffith's life there were many threads that show his dedication to justice. Similarly, on a cultural scale, there are English traditions of the rebels of seventeenth century England, the democratic communitarians and libertarians who were suppressed by Cromwell and King alike. As Christine Dann writes, we can choose the traditions we wish to build upon: *Winstanley and the suffragettes, whom I saw condemned in Lloyd George's handwriting in the British museum, were and are my people, the Britons I want to claim as ancestors.* (1991, p.51)

My identity as an Australian

More important than tracing the history of my ancestors, however, is the process of here and now. Becoming gubba involves the recognition that Indigenous Australians understand far more about us than we do about them, and perhaps even more than we know about ourselves.

Through resisting coming to terms with being white, we have not come to terms with our own place in this country. If we as gubbas take up the invitations from the indigenous peoples of this land to come to terms with our histories and our ongoing racism, then there is a hope for the development of truly Australian identities for non-indigenous people - identities based on justice: ... *white Australian terra nullus attitude right from the beginning of early settlement [sic] has led, I believe, to a spiritual numbness, Judith Wright's 'sightless shadow' at the centre of the national psyche.* (Scott 1991, p.181)

We have an opportunity to rid ourselves of this spiritual numbness. Part of such a process would involve acknowledging that much of what we refer to as Australian culture, when we mean white Australian culture, exists because of our relationship with the indigenous peoples of this land. Ted Egan writes: *'She'll be right' is an outlook we all like to think is 'typically Australian'. Well believe me, whether we like to acknowledge it or not, we have inherited this laconic approach to life from the first Australians.* (1994, p.74)

Similarly, parts of Australia's social landscape are due to the efforts of Aboriginal activism. The establishment of community legal and health centres and prison reforms are just a few examples where Indigenous Australian reforms have gone on to inspire changes that have benefited all Australians.

Coming to terms with the fact that we are the products of imperialism would hopefully also mean that we would demand an end to Australia's ongoing support of imperialism, be it in Bougainville, or East Timor, through selling uranium to the French, or allowing US bases on our soil.

Perhaps it would begin further processes of challenging racism. Becoming gubba is obviously not enough. White Australians such as myself are not racist only towards Indigenous Australians. The complexities involved in exploring how becoming gubba fits with challenging the racism we direct at other new arrivals to this country certainly need to be considered. For me, tapping into the histories of my people and the effects we have had on the indigenous peoples of this country, in some way locates me, names my experience. I hope this will open up space to further challenge the ways I participate in white supremacist practices.

Escape from prison history

> *Between convict and black, much blood is mingled in the soil of this ... island.*
> (Hughes 1988, p.120)

In order to truly come to terms with white peoples' crimes of the past against the indigenous peoples of this country, we will need to come to terms with ways of addressing wrongs that are not simply based on vengeance and punishment. This country was invaded so that it could be turned into a prison - a place where the working-class of England could be punished and hidden. Traditions of punishment, incarceration and vengeance still dominate our approaches to 'righting wrongs'.

It is of little surprise that in this context we white Australians do not want to admit to the wrongs carried out in our names. To take such responsibility, in our way of thinking, leads only to retribution and guilt. And when the crime is genocide there is all the more reason for denial. Indigenous Australians, however, seem to be attempting to show us that there are other ways forward - restorative ways, reconciliation. In the process perhaps we will realise that the ways in which we address crime in this country have far more to do with perpetuating race and class injustice than anything else.

It is no coincidence, in my mind, that white imperialism began in this country through the use of prison, that prisons are now a cornerstone in the continuing oppression of Indigenous Australians, and that the issue of punishment and vengeance needs to be addressed if we are ever to come to terms with our histories.

Responsibilities

Working in prisons means I am a white middle-class witness to gross injustice. By twists of fate I witness injustice that many people from my background do not see. It is a part of our privilege to have the option to cocoon ourselves from the results of injustice, such as poverty and incarceration. Being such a witness brings further responsibilities to reach out to my own kind, my people.

How to talk with other gubbas, other squareheads, how to support each other in facing the challenges of confronting racism and middle-class privilege, will, it seems, be all important. How we manage to resist trying to stand apart from other white people, other middle-class people, how we resist being more 'anti-racist than thou', will clearly be a measure of our commitment. As Chris McLean writes (in another context): *There are often very few opportunities for people to learn about these issues, and if we have had such opportunities, it is itself the result of privilege, and does not place us outside of our own culture* (1995, p.7). The processes of becoming squarehead, becoming gubba, are seeking to challenge white privilege and middle-class privilege. As a middle-class person, as a member of a colonising race, I must therefore constantly make myself open to the feedback of Indigenous Australians and working-class people with whom I work, about whether the explorations I am undertaking are of any benefit to them.

If we are ever to work in meaningful partnership across race and class divides then we as white middle-class professionals will need to be willing to listen to what those with whom we work really think of us and create the spaces in which to hear. Perhaps such conversations would open up space for us to work together.

There is no doubt that becoming squarehead, becoming gubba, is thoroughly enriching my life. Where once my life was consumed and emptied by the constant competition and isolation that is necessary to maintain privilege, now it is enriched by the sharing of stories, and the search for ways to resist. The challenges of those with whom I work have opened up new ways for me to understand my life. Entire histories and landscapes that were once invisible are now available for me to draw upon.

The conversations, friendships and relationships that have been a part of my life behind prison walls, have greatly shaped the person I now am. I hope such processes will continue. I hope they lead to action. From, me and others like me, I hope they lead to acts of redress. And together across differences I hope they lead to acts of creation - the creation of new histories and new futures.

References

Dann, C. 1991:
    'In love with the land.' In King, M. (ed), *Pakeha: The quest for identity in New Zealand*. Auckland, NZ: Penguin.
Egan, T. 1994:
    'Thinking in Australian.' In Graham, D. (ed), *Being Whitefella*. South Fremantle, Western Australia: Fremantle Arts Centre Press.
Elliot, 1994:
    'Whenever I tell you the language we use is a class issue, you nod your head in agreement - and then you open your mouth.' In Penelope, J. (ed*)*, *Out of the Class Closet: Lesbians Speak*. Freedom, CA: The Crossing Press.
Graham, Duncan, (ed), 1994:
    Being Whitefella. South Fremantle, Western Australia: Fremantle Arts Centre Press.
hooks, bell, 1994:
    Outlaw Culture. New York: Routledge.
Hughes, Robert, 1988:
    The Fatal Shore. London: Pan Books Ltd.
King, Michael, (ed) 1991:
    Pakeha: The quest for identity in New Zealand. Auckland, NZ: Penguin.
McEwen, C. 1994:
    'Growing up upper class.' In Penelope, J. (ed), *Out of the Class Closet: Lesbians Speak*. Freedom, CA: The Crossing Press.
McLean, C. 1995:
    'Speaking out from the dominant position.' *Comment, No.2*. Adelaide, South Australia: Dulwich Centre Publications.
Penelope, J. 1994:
    'Class and consciousness.' In Penelope, J. (ed), *Out of the Class Closet: Lesbians Speak*. Freedom, CA: The Crossing Press.
Scott, Rosie, 1991:
    'The trick of standing upright.' In King, M. (ed), *Pakeha: The quest for identity in New Zealand*. Auckland, NZ: Penguin.
Stir-Fry Productions, 1991:
    The Color of Fear. California.

P.S.:

This article is also to appear in an upcoming edition of the Dulwich Centre Newsletter on Prisons. As it is somewhat unusual to publish the same article twice, I wish to explain my reasons. I hope in each of the contexts it will be read rather differently and by different people.

I hope that in this book, surrounded by others' somewhat magical tales of work and life, it will read as the story of how my life has been enriched, moved, tumbled and tossed through my interactions with those with whom I work. I hope it may offer back to the members of a professional community whose ideas and passions have offered me so much, a little hope, a little light.

In the context of the prison newsletter, I hope my story will speak of my life where so often the lives of professionals in prisons remain invisible. I hope it will open up space to consider the complexities of working in prison and the political ramifications of imprisonment. Most importantly though, I hope the prison newsletter will be read not only by those who may read this book, but also those inside prisons.

Acknowledgements

The following people and communities have opened up space for me to consider my place in this culture, to explore the meanings of my life, and have in some way invited me to live and work with them to create new ways, new culture. I carry these connections and invitations with me, and they inform every conversation, every sentence.

'The Rollercoasters': Steve, Gary, Barry, Bob, Dave, John, Marshall, Don, Glen and Todd, for offering me trust, equity, the sharing of stories and for singing!

Bob, Gary, Barry, John, Ken, Danny, Brett & Kevin, for letting me know I am a squarehead and for the conversations - indeed heated discussions! They offered me hope of meaningful, respectful dialogue.

John W, whose letter to maintain connection will forever remain with me; John M, whose gentle trust honoured me; Archie, whose challenges and fire are still alive in my head; Bob, whose openness created pathways for me to travel; and Shane, whose energy within prison walls ripples and sparks.

Todd Gordon, with whom I shared stories, laughter, frustrations and heartache, who taught me through friendship and opened my heart to new ways of seeing.

Vicky Barrett, who shows me how spirits and sharing stories can bring us together, and Russel Sykes, whose determination and strength moves me on when my soul needs lifting.

Cheryl Gysin, for offering the strength of survival and the generosity of trusting me with her stories, and Wayne Jones for showing me that it is possible to unlock hearts of caged steel and to create friendship across lifetimes of difference.

All those involved in the Reclaiming Our Stories, Reclaiming Our Lives Project who offered me the most valuable of gifts - hope and ways of working together.

Victor Lewis (via technology!) for reaching my soul with his outrage, and for demanding that I ask myself what it means to be white.

Tony Magers, who brought me into the world of prisons and continues to journey with me, and Deirdre Hyslop who makes the journey possible by daring to care behind prison walls and bringing colour, light and laughter to a world in which it is often missing.

My family, for creating the space to imagine other ways of living and setting the example of taking risks in order to get there.

Cheryl White and Jane Hales and Maggie Carey and the communities to which they belong, for offering me friendship, for challenging my privilege, and for inviting me into worlds and ways of being that have revolutionised my life.

Samantha Wood, Rebecca Lee, David Newman, Mark Trudinger, Mark D'Astoli and all the others of us in this community that we are slowly building - a place from which we will speak and act, where our feet will be grounded, and from which we will reach out to others. I hope one day our community will offer as much to others as others have offered to me.

And finally to Lester Rigney, for reminding me of the importance of acknowledging the voices and spirits that I carry with me, in my day-to-day life, in my speaking, and in my writing.

Sharon Gollan

I was born at Point McLeay, a small Aboriginal Community south of Adelaide, South Australia. I am very proud of my heredity as a desendant of the Ngarrindjeri nation. I grew up mainly around this area, spending a majority of my growing-up years on an Aboriginal Reserve twenty minutes' driving time outside of Tailem Bend. I have happy and sad memories of my growing up years at this place more warmly-known to some members of the Aboriginal community as Mudangoon. This is the place where my mother was born, this was the place where she spent most of her growing up.

I am an avid fan and supporter of three wonderful young people: Mally Boy, Emily and Nikki. As you read on you will find that my seed of determination to keep going on has been at times watered by them, and at other times watered by my mother, father, brothers and sister.

But I cannot forget a little girl, crying and frightened at the time, praying and making a promise in the darkness of her room, making a promise about what she would do when she grows up. As this little girl was growing up, at times when she thought the promise was just too hard to keep, she just kept moving on, moving on, until she grew up to be Me. So now it is my turn to keep the promise for my children, for my family, for my people, and for me.

The Reasons For Why ...

Well I am sitting here thinking, where do I begin, how do I answer the question, 'As a practitioner, why do you continue to do what you do ?' My initial response would be, 'I do it for my children'. But I know that there are other reasons. I now have the opportunity and energy to think about it.

So what does it mean to keep on going? Well, one thing I know, there is more to it than how Rolf Harris projects it in the British Paints' commercial where he summarised it by saying something to the effect of: 'Trust British Paints? Sure can! They keep on keeping on.' So how do I keep on keeping on when battered by the storms? - the storms of prejudice, racism, cultural genocide, stereotyping and the many injustices imposed on myself, my family and my people, from the dominant culture.

To answer this question I will need to tell some stories of my past because I believe it was when I was just 7 years old that my determination, my strength, my courage to achieve started to grow. I remember making a decision to learn, to dream of growing·up and being special, being important, being different from what white people destined me to be.

I am the third-eldest child in a family of five. Of the many memories I carry I remember my strong determination to achieve. There was no way that I was going to accept what white people were saying that I would be or where I would end up. This determination became stronger when I started to have children because I wanted to make sure my children would not have to experience the hardship, the pain and the cruelty that I experienced growing up. I wanted them to have dreams and be in control of their own destiny; I wanted them to know who they were and grow proud.

Memories of my primary years at school were very painful. Even though I tried very hard I was not a good student. My parents were unable to provide support for me with my school work. However I was always strongly encouraged to do my work and attend school. I remember my older brothers being very good students, in particular the eldest. He was the one who became my competitor. I believe this was his way of encouraging me to keep on going through school. He would say things like, 'Well I've finished Year 10 (or Year whatever) - now can you beat that?' This was like waving a red flag to a bull because I would go for it. After a while I managed to do a lot more, but I always remembered what my brother did for me, so one day the role was reversed and I was the one to say to him: 'Well I've finished ... So when are you going to finish your teaching degree?'; it was my turn to encourage my brother to complete his degree. Today he is a school principal, and I am a manager. However, at this time I knew the competition had finished because for me the competition become a different game and the competitor a different person.

By this time you may be wondering when I will get to the question of 'As a practitioner why do you continue to do what you do?' - or maybe I am still wondering how I am going to respond to the question. However, I do feel a sense of excitement that I have begun to answer the question. But I am at a different point where I am thinking how can I now, in only a few words, cover the next passage of my life which is vital to why I keep moving on.

Like the time when my first-born, as a 5 year old, was moved to the back of the class, or my second pride and joy was called 'Abo', or my sweetest baby at 6 years old was stared at and then asked, 'Is that your mummy?' by a person looking back and forth from Nikki to me. Now by this time in my life I had learnt not to think negative thoughts when someone would stare or glare at me, i.e. thoughts like: 'Why are they staring at me? It must be because I am black', but today even that type of stare is all right with me because I have replaced the negative association of this stare with a positive one: 'Yes, I am black - WOW!'

However, on this day it was particularly hard not to think negative thoughts, particularly when the person continued to stare, glancing from Nikki to me, then said, 'Oh, is she adopted?' I just smiled, grabbed Nikki's hand and said, walking out of the shop, 'No, she is my baby'. Then I had to reassure Nikki when she asked me, 'What's adoption mean?', that she was not adopted, that she belonged to her Mum and Dad, her brother and her sister. But, more importantly, she is Ngarringjeri, she is black, which I could see was very important to Nikki.

From here it seems to go on and on, storm after storm, backwards and forwards. But, I chose to go on. So why? Maybe it was because of the time when I was giving a presentation to Rotarians, hoping to raise sponsorship monies for Aboriginal youth to attend a culture camp in Victoria. I was speaking about the importance of our culture when I heard a muffled comment from behind me, 'They should be lined up and shot'. I remember turning to see who it was, taking a picture of the person, and saying to myself: 'So you are my competitor!!! Now for the challenge', and I moved on.

Or was it the time on graduation day as I was walking across the stage at the Festival Theatre to collect my award, all dressed up in my cloak and cap, and I heard this strong voice across the crowd yell out, 'Good on ya mum!' It was Emily, then just 8 years old. What a feeling it gave me in that split second! I remember having flashbacks to my childhood years, remembering some of the other voices, both good and bad. Most of all I remembered my Dad who had passed away, and my brother who died in police custody, and I thought that I would burst - they were with me on that day right up there on the stage. And I moved on. Even as I write this I feel tears of joy and a sigh of heaviness, so I will just stand back from it for a moment, but I know I will go on.

The heaviness is there because I guess I am now at the next passage of my life, my next biggest moment to share with my father, brother and brother, sister, mother, Malcolm, Mally Boy, Emily and Nikki. For this moment was the marking of different challenges, for now I would begin a journey to challenge systems. Systems built by the dominant culture that were there to benefit me, my family and Aboriginal people.

I wonder about the sigh of heaviness. Why has it crept in? I guess because it has been a long and sometimes lonely journey. A journey where I have found myself at times feeling lost and incomplete. So tired, just wanting to sleep, or at times just wanting to walk away, walk away ...

Walk away and be on my own, stop having to watch the white person for learning. Learning what to say and how to say it in order to gain what you need for yourself, for your family, for your people. For some of you readers, you may not understand what I am talking about here but, being born black, I was always having to prove my self-worth to white people. Working harder, much harder than if you were born white. Making sure I got it right, knowing if I didn't that it would also reflect back on my people, my family, my children. It was during these times that it would get lonely, where you would feel isolated from whites because you were black, but, more importantly, a painful isolation from your people, being thought of as a traitor when all the time you were in camouflage learning all about your opponent. But you keep going because you have seen it working, you have experienced the win for your people, your family and for yourself. You have just been involved in an important meeting which has resulted in a excellent project for your community, or you have just come from a Christmas party organised for Nunga kids with a Nunga Father Christmas, or you have just corrected someone from being racist, or you receive an award acknowledging your commitment to your people. The pain is replaced by determination: determination to see more happy faces, more projects, programmes in your community; determination to see your mother's and your father's faces shine with pride; determination to feel the win. I do not just mean the feeling of exhilaration that comes from a win like at football or the Olympics, but I refer here to the feeling of peace that comes with this win.

There are many times when I ask myself the questions: 'Why do you do it Sharon? Why do you move on? Why do you keep doing it? Why don't you just take things easy, step back and leave it to someone else? Why do you put yourself through so much pain?' Because at times, when going on, that's what it brings your way - pain and sadness. This is where I am right now ... It seems such a long time since the beginning of writing this article. Since then I have been hit by another storm, another battle of resistance. So I wonder how I can bring this experience of the storm and the determination to move on into the article to share with you. So I am thinking, 'How do I write about it, when in reality I have to move through it?' So I asked Leela to interview me, determined to keep going on. Determined to stay truthful to my promise at 7 years old. Determined to feel a sense of achievement and peace.

So here we are together, sharing in the interview I had with Leela about why I continue to do what I do - this awkward space that I'm in at the moment ...

Sharon: I was thinking about how I could actually bring the space that I am in right this minute into the article, because in relation to the question, it's very much where I am now - but in trying to write about it, I find it too hard.

Leela: So you're hoping that maybe we can just kind of talk it through, so the space that you're in at the moment - there's a link between that and that question of *Bedtime Stories* of 'Why do you keep going as a practitioner and how do you keep going?' What do you think the link is?

Sharon: The link is actually - it's responding to it, it is actually doing the moving on ... for yourself, but in other ways it's also for others that you, as a practitioner, as a person, are doing the moving on for. It's also a different feeling from what I've noticed before when at these crossroads, at these times where I've been in this space. I would like to highlight the difference.

Leela: So there's a different feeling now, on this crossroad, than in the past?

Sharon: Yes. The determination is still there, but I don't feel as low or lonely. And I'm still so determined to move on, but what I have now is a feeling of not being so alone in moving on. I feel more encouraged, I believe, to reach out to continue the work that I am doing, particularly for Aboriginal people. Whereas before I had a sense of feeling as though I was alone and more that it was about me.

Leela: Moving on feeling not so alone ... What else is different about your experience of being at this crossroad?

Sharon: Well, the moving on or being entitled to move on - because of the past feelings of not being able to, that I'm not worthy - I had a lot of conditioning of negative voices of myself as a person moulded in me by people of the dominant culture, which made it hard for me to actually want to move on. It took a lot more energy or a lot more of myself to get up to go on. This time I've noticed the difference. Like I've noticed that, even though it's still hard, I have different voices, voices from Camp Coorong, the United States, New Zealand, that confirm for me different messages. Messages that have made me connect with who I really am. Messages of my strengths, my courage, my love and passion for my people, for my family. Messages that I now believe in, that it's not all about me - that I am worthless and bad - but it is about the systems. And, like the systems, there are people out there who are racist - it is not about me being always defensive or paranoid. So I now believe that I am worthy of moving on. So I do.

Leela: So there's something about the work you've been doing, and the connections you've been making through Camp Coorong and through New Zealand, people in the United States - there's something about those connections and those experiences that have helped you to shift from those internal voices of self criticism, to somehow seeing it outside of you and much broader?

Sharon: Yes.

Leela: So what do you think it was about those experiences that helped you to do that?

Sharon: I connect with - I guess it was listening, it was actually during the process of the listening team, like when the team were reflecting. I heard that people on the reflecting team actually heard what we were talking about and they didn't judge it or label it, but actually talked about the strength and the courage that I had - hearing those messages sort of made me connect to the person. I was saying, 'Wow, that was pretty extraordinary'. So I was able to, and the other family members were able to, start hearing and feeling and connecting up with the strengths and the courage that we all have that we didn't know or realise that we have.

Leela: So what was important to you about hearing it from somebody else? Like, how was that different? Like, before you had to be your own team?

Sharon: Yes.

Leela: Something shifted. So I'm wondering what was important about hearing it from other people outside yourself that helped make that shift?

Sharon: I guess what was important was that I was starting to feel that people would believe me, like, before you would be crying out about either yourself or experiences of my people and the experiences of whatever - that is, if it's racism or whatever, the sadness that you were experiencing was being believed. Whereas before you had to keep on convincing, defending it, instead of just having people listen and hear, or you would have to label it, or be labelled.

Leela: Is this the first time that you felt believed by people from the dominant culture? Was Camp Coorong the first time that you felt really believed and understood and acknowledged?

Sharon: It's the first time that I was able to believe ... There were a lot of people that were in my life prior to Camp Coorong, from the dominant culture, who I regarded as friends and who I still regard today as friends, but I'm not sure if they actually really connected with the pain, or with the sadness. And never connected in and talked about your strengths. There were some who did, but I didn't actually believe, I mean, I didn't know who they were talking about when they'd say to me that 'You're a strong woman'. I remember one person who was saying to me, 'You know, Sharon, you're a very strong person', and she looked at me and she knew that I didn't know what she was talking about. And I could say I didn't know. But after Camp Coorong, and hearing from the team about the experiences that I experienced of hearing about the different experiences of other family members from Camp Coorong, it started adding up. So I guess something just clicked. It was a pretty extraordinary experience. It was like a feeling of being rebirthed. It was just fantastic ...

Leela: Because I guess I'm thinking: well, there must have been lots of changes happening because when you spoke of that friend who said, you know, 'Sharon, you're a really strong woman', and she could recognise that, but there was kind of like no rich ground for that to fall on because you didn't believe it. But somehow during Camp Coorong, those words could fall on ready ground and so that the feelings could then grow. So I guess I'm wondering how you prepared the ground yourself, or what helped prepare that ground, for you to be able to hear those words and believe them?

Sharon: I guess my determination of wanting to believe that you are an OK person and that you are worthwhile and so get rid of the old feelings. And I guess there was a big part of me - because of the giving that I gave to people from the dominant culture, I just wanted something back. And so it was like screaming from the top of a mountain that I want something back - 'I have given you enough'.

Leela: I guess I'm sitting here thinking, Sharon that's a long time to wait for that sort of acknowledgement and understanding - to have that need as we all do, to be loved and to be recognised, and all of those years where not only have you experienced the opposite, experiences which fed self-hatred or a sense of worthlessness. Yet Camp Coorong - that was an experience that you were able to believe. I'm wondering how you were able to keep that seed of self-love even alive and for it not to be, to wait for Camp Coorong to be watered. Does that make sense?

Sharon: Yes it does. Up until Camp Coorong the watering happened with family, and the watering happened with my brothers, my sister and my father. I didn't know otherwise. I didn't have any expectations from others, particularly from people of the dominant culture. But I guess the beginning where I started to feel that the water was running out was when Dad died, and then when Stephan died, because when he died that's when a big part of me just wanted to walk away from it, like I just had a strong sense of thinking, 'I don't want to do this any more': continue working and believing that things would change with white people. So I had a sense of running out. However, what made me move on from a sense of feeling that I didn't want to do it anymore was hearing and remembering some of the memories of Stephan saying that 'I'm proud of you Sis, don't worry about me', I could actually visualise and hear him saying things like, 'It'll be all right'.

Leela: It's like his spirit could water you - you were having a very dry season. His pride in you ...

Sharon: So that gave me the urge, to go on - I had a very strong feeling that he would just not want me to give in - to keep on fighting and also knowing, with Mally Boy, Emily and Nikki, I had to go on for them so that gave me enough to move. I didn't want to believe the dominant cultural idea of having to let go of Stephan in order to move on.

Leela: So there was some part of you where also those ideas didn't fit. That you have such a strong wanting to have Stephen in your life and in your children's lives and in your sister's life, that you didn't totally buy into that, that way of thinking about death and spirituality?

Sharon: I was already starting to question other parts of the dominant culture a lot by this stage. But in my questioning, and because I didn't have a lot of positives about myself, I felt I couldn't question. I mean, surely you can't question a psychiatrist or you can't question these people from the dominant culture, like, they know it all, they have the right - white is right.

Leela: White is right?

Sharon: Yes. And who are you to question these people? So, I mean, even though I had doubts, the other negative voices would just stop me from really challenging. But there was enough in me to ... challenge. It was like searching, telling myself I couldn't be totally wrong. So there was a part of me that kept searching.

Leela: So that sort of quality - that questioning part of you that wasn't prepared to go with 'white is right' - it sounds like it teamed up with this kind of inner-knowing that you knew that this wasn't the right way for you to go. What would you call it - a knowing, or what, that matched up with that questioning?

Sharon: Well, I guess because there was some experience of white stories that had been sprung, I used to ask my father whether black people resisted. And why did we allow white people to come in and take over our land - didn't we fight? And during schooling there were no stories about our fighting. And Dad would say, 'Yes', but he wouldn't tell me too much about what happened, and I think that was part of his protecting me. But it was when I was studying just six, seven years ago that I actually found out that there was strong resistance by Aboriginal people. That our people were just amazing, our ancestors did some amazing things in relation to resistance. So in hearing that, I was actually sitting in lectures and hearing those stories, like I remember feeling, like, so this was what Dad was talking about. And I remember feeling a strong sense of sadness because I never was able to say to him, or have the opportunity to say to him, 'How amazing', but, most of all, I never had the opportunity to say, 'I believe you' and tell him, 'I'm sorry, Dad, for disbelieving in you'. And so, because they'd then been sprung, that just gave me enough opening to keep thinking, 'Wow, well what else is behind there?' I don't know how or what, but it certainly connects up very much with why I keep searching still. The secret's out.

Leela: Searching still and the secret's out. And so the connection between the searching and opening the lid on this secret and letting it out - the connection between that and why you keep going ...

Sharon: So I can let my people know. Because there's so many of us that really believe that things only exist for white people or that we are not worthy. I'm just wanting to let them know that it's not true - that's what keeps me going. And for my kids. That they believe in themselves and that they don't have to be white to be able to do whatever they dream of doing. That dreams are not just only for white people. That we can have dreams too.

Leela: When you first started talking, you talked about moving on but not feeling alone this time and moving on to challenging systems, systems of institutionalised racism. And I'm wondering if some of what you just named about searching and the secret's out - I'm wondering if that's a part of your next step of moving on ...

Sharon: Yes, I've got white voices now too.

Leela: Do you want to help me understand that - you've got white voices too?

Sharon: I have the white voices of the reflecting team from Camp Coorong and voices from other people from the dominant culture who believe in me and who know about the secret. I know that these voices are standing with me. So if the old voices of negativeness question me and my rights as an Aboriginal woman, I know who to go to, or I know how to challenge them and how to sort through them. It's like building an army now when stepping out. I am not alone - I have those voices now. Knowing this helps.

Leela: The circle is getting wider now, the circle can include some white people who can - again, I think that words are failing me as well ... It's like somehow you don't have to do all of the work on your own; that in connecting with some of these people - it's also about white people doing some of the work ourselves. I don't know if that is my agenda, and I've put a meaning into the conversation, or whether it fits for you too.

Sharon: Well, what fits for me is that by listening to and respecting my stories, by respecting me, they in turn have respected and listened to the stories of Stephan and Dad and of all the family members at Camp Coorong. For me that's what really matters. Yes that's what it is: it's the respect and the respecting of the stories and of Stephan and the love. I know that, in loving and respecting me, they love and respect my family ...

Leela: So I'm wondering if the passport is love and respect - so unless those white people actually love and respect Stephan through both you and your family, and respect the Aboriginal community ... As we're talking now about love and respect, it somehow feels like it's touched something or brought some strong feelings up for you ...

Sharon: Yes, because he deserved to be loved and that's what makes me happy. People may not have physically met him but through me they have - and in welcoming me into their lives and in loving me, in hearing my stories and respecting my stories - to me that's saying that in fact they love him too. And they love and respect my father, my children, my mother. That's what angers me: the memories of my father who was treated with so much disrespect from people from the dominant culture and the systems. Having to go and get government orders for food or clothes for us - he did all those things for us for our survival. And he was treated with little respect. I guess that's what catches it all, that they can now have that respect ...

Leela: So something about through you refusing to give up, and through you moving on - that respect can flow back to them in the way they never received in their living lives. Through your determination to continue to move on, they get to have some of that love and respect that they never received.

Sharon: So that's what keeps me going. And it makes me happy. My love for my family, for my people, and the importance of respect for them, just keeps me hanging on, keeps me going on - in nurturing that, then that nurtures me ...

Leela: Again I think of the circle of how that sense of the love and the respect that you are working for Stephan and for your father and other Aboriginal people - it's like that also nurtures you. So it becomes a circle rather than a line, where you are giving back to them. It's knowing they are feeling loved and respected also nurtures you and waters you.

Sharon: So I know now that, when I'm at the crossroads, I'm watered enough to just say, 'OK, it's just going to be for a little while. Hang on and remember your dreams as a child. Remember the stories when growing up, remember the feeling, the experience of the win, not just that exhilaration win, but that feeling of peace win - the feeling of freedom ...

I am really happy to have got to this stage of the story. It helps to know why I keep going on. Sometimes you can get lost in the doing, and the doing then can get lost in the why you do it. Prior to writing this story I had a sense of why I kept going, but I now have a stronger more clearer message as to why I do it. The knowing now will help in the doing. I know there will be more storms to come that may delay the doing, but I have this story, and remembering my dreams as a child, remembering the stories when growing up, remembering the promise, will determine me even more to move on and to keep doing it. And if I slide too far away from the doing I know someone will always be there to reach out and remind me of the reasons for why, and help me to move on to keep doing it ... *GOODNIGHT.*

Acknowledgements

I must thank many people for their support in helping complete this paper. To my family for their love and their support. To my mother, father, brothers and sister. To the many faces I have come to know and love through the connections with Camp Coorong, from North, South, East and West, across the seas and inland. To Robyn, Kath, and all my friends and colleagues who have stood by me and, at times, in front of me.

I particularly wish to thank Leela Anderson and Cheryl White for the opportunity to be a part of *Bedtime Stories*. A special thank you to you, Leela - despite your busy schedule, you made yourself available to interview me which encouraged and inspired me to move on and complete this paper.

To Malcolm, Mally Boy, Emily, Nicole, Mum, Dad, Lawrie, Stevie, Debbie, Phillip, and to my people and the families who shared in our grief and sadness at Camp Coorong, this story would never have been without you - I thank you ...

This Story this Place I dedicate to you Dad, and to you my brother Stephan ... hello fellow ...